D1796038

AWE
IN
ACTION

Plus est en vous que vous pensez

There Is More in You Than You think.

"This book prompts powerful thinking that will trigger leaders in education into action – in a world where curriculum is being squeezed, and wellbeing in the communities we serve severely challenged by lack of investment, the type of work you are doing will prove, in some cases, no less than life saving... "

Guy Shears – Executive Principal (CEO), Central RSA Academies Trust, National Leader of Education

"Awe in Action gives us many ways to reflect on our student narratives and therefore improve them by making them more memorable, authentic, purposeful and inspiring. The writing here captures the backbone of Expeditionary Learnings' purpose. A valuable contribution."

Gwyn ap Harri – CEO, XP Schools Trust

"An insightful and engaging book that makes an important link between outdoor adventurous education and the cultivation of practical wisdom in young people. With Awe in Action, Kevin Long demonstrates the importance of emotion in learning and places a specific focus on the character virtues and values that might be developed through high impact experiences."

Dr Tom Harrison - Head of Education, Jubilee Centre for Character & Virtue, University of Birmingham

"...There is some very powerful writing in this book which strikes a real chord...it brings together a range of ideas to express a powerful philosophy and I hope that it inspires many readers to take action!" - **Dr Randall Williams, Chair of English Outdoor Council (Retired)**

"An inspiring read. An important reminder of the benefits of a truly enriching curriculum. Powerful and engaging."

Richard Gill, CEO, Arthur Terry Learning Partnership, National Leader of Education

"Wonderfully articulates the underlying drivers and motivations for why the #iwill campaign and its partners are so passionate about seeing more social action embedded in the culture and practice of schools. This book will no doubt be a valuable contribution within the ongoing debate about rediscovering the wider moral purpose of education."

Chloe Donovan, Education Officer, Step-up to Serve. #IWill Campaign.

AWE
IN
ACTION
DELIVERING HIGH IMPACT LEARNING

KEVIN LONG

AWE IN ACTION

Copyright © Kevin P. Long, 1.1.2017

The Moral right of Kevin Long to be identified as the author of this work has been asserted in accordance with the Copyright, Design and Patents Act of 1988.

First Published 2018

The Outward Bound Trust
Hackthorpe Hall, Penrith, Cumbria CA10 2HX

ISBN- 13: 978-0-9547782-2-4
ISBN-10: 0-9547782-2-7

A Catalogue record of this book is available
from the British Library

All Rights Reserved

Except for the quotation of short passages of criticism and review, no part of this book may be reproduced in any form, by photocopying or by any electronic or mechanical means, Including information storage or retrieval systems, without the prior written permission from both the copyright owner and the publisher of this book.

Printed and bound for

THE OUTWARD BOUND TRUST

ENDORSEMENT

Now, more than ever, we need a book like this to remind us that education is not about test scores — it is about bringing out the best in students as learners, citizens, and human beings. We don't have to choose between instilling virtuous and courageous character in students and building their academic skills. When students are engaged in challenging, meaningful work; when they can contribute through their work to a better world; and when they are expected to treat themselves and others with respect and kindness, they are inspired to succeed in all realms, in school and life.

This book describes the beautiful vision and heritage of educator Kurt Hahn and Outward Bound, and how the spirit of that work can be brought into schools to revitalize purpose and success for teachers and students.

Ron Berger
Chief Academic Officer
EL Education

FOREWORD

This book is dedicated to those countless educators who believe in the potential of all children and who set out to create awe in their lives. On behalf of The Outward Bound Trust, I am delighted to be writing the forward to this book.

Kevin Long has given a voice to the concept that lies at the very heart of the Outward Bound movement. There is more to education than the goings-on in a classroom. A great education equips a young person with more than a bunch of academic certificates. It is also vital that all young people are given the opportunity to be set ablaze emotionally in response to a physical or mental challenge, to embrace an element of risk and to feel the elation of approaching a mountain top. It is through such peak experiences that we may unlock the great potential within us all.

Of course, within Outward Bound we take this very literally. Journeying in the mountains can be awe inspiring and you really do approach a mountain top! Instilling resilience, raising aspiration and getting young people to engage emotionally are the inevitable consequences of a well delivered Outward Bound course.

There are other means to the same end. A young person performing in a play, singing a solo at a concert or opening the batting in a cricket match will also learn hugely about challenge, risk and the possibility of elation. To get to their mountain top, they too will have to dig deep.

But what all of these things have in common is that they are intense and viscerally lived experiences. They can unlock the moment of grace when a young person realises there is much more in them than they think. They can be awesome.

Nick Barrett
Chief Executive Officer
The Outward Bound Trust

December 2017

PREFACE

Think of the enthusiasm and wonder and joy that awe-filled experiences bring to our children. Awe is not a term heard very often in schools, but it's potential is vast. Too many children are growing up without sufficient experiences to build their strength in virtues, sense of service or collective responsibility. With the crisis of values in modern society there is a desperate need to readdress this. Awe is an emotion that has the potential to inspire pro-social action, increase wellbeing and raise aspirations for the greater good. This emotion has the potential to support a change in education.

We all have a propensity to experience and create awe. I argue here that we are best able to achieve this by being fully active participants in life. We can be moved by the moral excellence in others and by our own courage in action. Each transformative moment works to redraw the map slightly and helps each of us find our own way. By doing so we grow new possibilities- as ripples of goodness- through our own life's actions. This is *flourishing*, and it is awe in action.

We can all be inspired by stories of young people who have made a difference in the world such as Malala Yousafzai, Stephen Sutton, Logan McKerrow and Craig Kielburger, or Ryan Hreljac and most recently Emma Gonzalez.[1] As activists for education, health, disability and child rights, respectively they contributed to a cause much bigger than themselves. In fact all children are activists;

they too want to be able to make a difference. They want to be heard, to share their discoveries, to explore and wander in their learning. They have such insatiable levels of energy, a restlessness that constantly needs to be used up in exploration and discovery. Their energy for doing things has need for harnessing in a purposeful constructive way or it will be left to grow in frustration. When a child is listened to and respected, they grow in confidence and kindness. When we empower children to improve in their own world, we allow them to fulfil their potential.

We live in such uncertain times, a world wearied by atrocity, one beset with human crises, polarisation and societal stresses not seen since the early twentieth century. Now, more than ever, we must support our young in developing a resilience in the face of uncertainty and the courage to act on goodness despite ignorance, intolerance and irrational dogma. This work attempts to answer the question: *How can educators help cultivate an engaged and meaningful life? A life in which children feel inspired to be their best selves, to feel part of something bigger than themselves.* The answer argues for the importance of active powerful learning experiences. The writing belies a strong desire to encourage prosocial and humanitarian values in learning- an education for the whole child. There are too few opportunities to make contributions in school; which makes school feel isolated and irrelevant. By enabling students to find a greater connection we allow them to enjoy their learning and make valuable contributions to their community. Connecting classrooms with the purpose of a greater cause impels deeper learning itself.

The essays in this book look at how the emotional response to experiences can condition our action and in turn form the habits of our character. Just as we are moved by witnessing excellence in others, they may similarly get inspiration from us. The 'other-praising' emotions of gratitude, admiration and moral elevation, play an important role in our living. The feelings of admiration inspire compassion, prosocial values and impel us to action for the pursuit of worthy service. Inspiring children to help others is the most effective way to promote responsibility, empathy, and self-esteem. It is an effective way to address the narcissism of adolescence. Through action, children feel that they can have an impact on their world. They become hopeful about the future and this helps put them on a path to a life lived in compassionate connection with others.

My hope is that you will digest this short work and through your own practice bring to use the message provided. You will take away different things and apply in your own manner. The fact is that you and your children will be the doers, the changers, the influencers. If there is to be any merit, it will be yours. If I have kindled ideas within you and should they be taken as your starting point from which to engage and grow your students, then this work has been a worthwhile undertaking.

Kevin Long,
December 2017

CONTENTS

Table of Contributions

Table of Figures:

INTRODUCTION

*"...it is culpable neglect not to impel young people
into health giving experiences"* Kurt Hahn[1]

There are positive experiences in life that endure. *Defining moments* that we might repeatedly return to long after the passing of time, that live on in our memory. Such experiences become part of the fabric of our identity, they help us tell our story. Perhaps it is in overcoming difficulty or situations that provide opportunities for selflessness, service and learning. They may carry a meaning to us which we rely upon for guidance or support; they live on in us somehow and become interwoven with our values.

It is my intention to convey the potential for such experiences in learning. The moral emotions of awe, elevation,* admiration and gratitude have an important role to play in inspiring learning, in building virtues of character and in guiding self-development.

Examples of courage, kindness and resilience can bring the delicate and very human capacity for awe to mind. These emotions impel us towards prosocial action[†] ... and that action is compassion.

---

* *This is not a common term, the term: Moral elevation is defined later in the chapter titled "A Catalyst for Caring". Suffice to say it is an emotion that's closely related to awe, is elicited when witnessing excellence in virtue and often results the individual feeling optimistic about humanity and creates an enhanced desire to become a better person.*

[†] *Voluntary behaviours that benefit others such as helping, sharing, donating, co-operating, and volunteering*

1

Experiences that dwarf us, that make us feel tiny and insignificant have been eliciting powerful emotions since our species earliest days. In *The Outdoor Educators Guide to Awe*, the focus was on the emotion as far it lends itself to positive transformative learning. Evoked by experiences predominantly outside of our influence or control.[2] We attribute an agency to powerful, beautiful or overwhelming phenomena. In our explanation for such experiences we have the classical view of Awe in that the experiences assure us of some greater power at work to which we are indebted. It rests on the premise of an agency outside of our own control. We might feel indescribable awe and wonder, but it is not always consistently clear what to do with this intense feeling.

As educators and pragmatists, we should be interested in those experiences where the locus of agency impacts upon our own personal capacity. When the attribution of peak experiences come from recognising the potential in others, we may become more purposeful and better reasoned agents of change for the common good- in doing so realising our own best selves.

In this collection of essays, the focus is narrowed down to those transformational moments from the excellence we see in others and from the good we perceive in ourselves.[3] Here the essays concern the facilitation of Awe through personal or collaborative experiences, in and through our own action. When, through collaborative effort, we realise the potential in others and the greater good when all together, we are moved deeply. Insights

2

occur that light up the latent potential within ourselves.‡ This is Awe in action.

Through the impact of action there is potential to change our everyday selves and our world views. If we can be awed by the power of one, then we can raise our expectations for the possibilities of what can be achieved together.

In considering moments of outstanding achievement we might likely think of the great occasions of human deed or collaboration such as exploring the frontiers. Learning of such feats no doubt has the potential to elevate and fuel an inspiration, a sense of wonder in us. Yet the endeavour does not have to be amongst the most prominent achievements in human history. Breaking sound barriers, reaching the highest summits, or building the greatest bridges are indeed incredible, but we too can be elevated though an uncommon act in the every day. Consider moments where-

- Humanity and courage shown by overcoming personal adversity.
- Dedication of service and patient loyalty
- Models of wisdom, charity and example.
- Moving acts of rescue, bravery and heroism.

---

‡ *Powerful experiences can be created by the process of rising to a challenge which the student initially thought beyond them (often supported and enhanced by the group interaction). Leading to a positive reappraisal of self-worth and potential.*

3

This monograph does not extol the benefits of cure-alls, populist themes or miracle interventions in education. It is concerned with relevant and *connected* approaches to learning and pupil engagement. First and foremost, it is concerned with values. The case presented is a commitment to using experiential learning[4] as an important means to supporting the development of young people, not in a way that dominates or provides an easy solution but one that seeks to compliment other strategies within the social educational context.[5]

The following essays look at the benefits to ourselves, our children and our society with this in mind. It is through these challenges that I provide hope for your practice and encouragement for change.

Part One addresses the positive emotions of elevation, awe, admiration and appreciation. It concerns the emotional response and importance of pro-social emotions in learning– our students are not inert recipients in their learning. Part Two proposes a set of executive skills that can be developed to help build qualities and virtues that condition action for challenging situations. These essays address the importance of the prosocial benefits of emotion and the importance of moral elevation for action.

Part Three introduces high impact learning and considers steps towards introducing Expeditionary Learning into the traditional schooling framework. Here our attention is drawn to what can be done in schools to achieve greater autonomy and self-directed learning. The premise is that social opportunities make a direct contribution to the expansion of human capabilities and virtues for a better quality of life. This is especially important when considering the gap in social mobility and the poverty of opportunity that exists in many communities. With this in mind, the essays argue for more connection and a better "grasp of the world" through an ethic of service in school life. School is not a place apart and education does not stop at the school gates. The philosophy of expeditionary learning is offered from an angle relevant to a school in the United Kingdom with a state mandate. The potential of Adventurous Learning for increasing engagement with challenge is considered. Whilst the educational credibility of alternative approaches may still remain unclear with many school leaders, I hope to convey here that adventure is an intrinsic part of high impact learning. Complex non-linear situations afford the opportunity for complex learning and breakthroughs. Chapters such as Engaging with Challenge will highlight the real tragedies of our educational system – the withdrawal and disengagement of pupils and the "switching off" of their natural ability to learn. The elements of adventure may not be thoroughly discussed here, but suffice to say that uncertainty, risk, discovery, resourcefulness and potential need not be foreign concepts to the classrooms. Perhaps the foremost task is to first understand that an authentic Adventurous Learning approach is not "a nice to have option"- it is essential for every learning community.

"We need to think more carefully through the body in order to cultivate ourselves and edify our students because true humanity is not a mere genetic given but an educational achievement in which body, mind, and culture must be thoroughly integrated." - Richard Shusterman[6]

PART ONE

FINDING AWE IN ACTION

THE AWE IN ACTION

"When any ...act of charity or of gratitude, for instance, is presented either to our sight or imagination, we are deeply impressed with its beauty and feel a strong desire in ourselves of doing charitable and grateful acts also" Thomas Jefferson, Letter to Robert Skipwith, 1771

The word "awesome" has become so heavily used in every day casual conversation today that it has lost almost all of its gravitas. Back in August of 2014, Jill Shargaa did a TED Talk about today's rampant overuse of the word awesome. Hers was a humorous plea to stop this elevation of the mundane. "If everything is awesome," Shargaa says, "then there are no highs or lows, no dynamic." The truly awesome encounters in life are typically uncommon – indeed the experiences we have that are somehow magnificent and powerful are given additional impact by their scarcity.

Research in psychology is beginning to show that the kinds of objects, environments, and people that elicit feelings of awe affect our behaviours and even protect our health. The message of recent findings is clear, if you want to improve your life, go do something awesome. An "awe experience" increases our "empathetic currency" and makes us more willing to connect with others in a prosocial manner. What's more, we can get *a double dose of awe*, in finding inspiration in our ability to go beyond our limitations, as well as the inspiration from the personal experience. The experience adds to the fabric of our identity – in recollection, we relive the positive experiences and continue to benefit from them.

In the 1960s, Abraham Maslow had looked closely at "peak experiences" – described as "especially joyous and exciting moments" in life, involving sudden feelings of intense happiness and wellbeing, wonder and awe, perhaps involving an awareness or perceiving the world from a new perspective. Maslow argued that "peak experiences" should continue to be studied and cultivated, so that they can be introduced to those who have never had them or who resist them, "providing them a route to achieve personal growth, integration, and fulfilment." There has been a resurgence of interest, that corresponds with Abraham Maslow's work – such as Paul Puff's research in 2015 to describe the prosocial benefits of experiencing awe.

There is something egalitarian about a sense of wonder and awe. Peak experiences are universal in that the emotional response is part of our biology.[1] We can all feel the power of nature regardless of our socio-economic status - if only given the opportunity.

The impact of peak experiences can be elicited in a single moment and yet endure a lifetime. As a life enhancing experience, awe and elevation have a powerful transformational capacity which leads to wellbeing, health and happiness. In moral elevation, admiration, awe and gratitude we have a family of powerful prosocial emotions that inspire us into action.

The focus is narrowed down to those transformational and expansive moments that stem from the excellence seen in others and from transcending our own limitations. In doing so, the powerful feelings of elevation, of awe and wonder can be found and elicited in ourselves more often than we might think.[2]

Perception is more than the mere physical stimulation of sense organs. It also produces mental imagery, visual and otherwise. Through episodic memory we can re-create feelings of awe through a sense elevation. Imagination makes possible all our thinking about what is, what has been, and, perhaps most important, what might be. Concepts such as embodied cognition and predictive processing are revolutionizing our understanding of such psychological phenomena.[3]

Stories of awe are timeless. They do not have to be our own to cue a sense of reverence and moral elevation. We can be moved in admiration and inspired by the everyday examples of others. Consider people at work - such as the surgeon at Alder Hey Children's Hospital, whom I learnt, puts the child patient at ease and leaves them in wonder as he tells them everything they had for breakfast just by pressing on their tummy. Now the child is no longer worried – "what an amazing man will be looking after my operation". Or the nurse who dealt with that most unusual request in a trusting and kind way – a man wanting to visit a particular place on the ward. Later she learnt that the bed they stood by was where his son died. He took out his GPS to mark the spot where his son left this earth- so he could visit and sit at the spot in the garden once the new hospital was built. In the decisions, we make and the actions we take we have a greater impact than we may presently know.

There is a greater self, a footprint which stems from our deeds. The message is that the potential for awe is in our hands, every day.

We instinctively attribute an agency to powerful, beautiful or overwhelming phenomena, especially those evoked by experiences outside of our influence or control Experiences that dwarf us, that make us feel tiny and insignificant, have triggered a core emotion deep within us since our species earliest days. In our explanation for such experiences we have the classical view of Awe, the emotion assures us of some greater agency. The feeling of reverence that arises in us drives us to do better for others. Consider John Muir's example of being awed by the mountains and by his discoveries.

"We are now in the mountains and they are in us, kindling enthusiasm, making every nerve quiver, filling every pore and cell of us. Our flesh-and-bone tabernacle seems transparent as glass to the beauty about us, as if truly an inseparable part of it, thrilling with the air and trees, streams, and rocks, in the waves of the sun — a part of all nature, neither old nor young, sick nor well, but immortal."

Out of those experiences of awe, Muir began to write and inspire others and form the Sierra Club, and eventually inspire the creation of the state and national park system. Dacher Keltner[4], professor of psychology at the University of California, Berkeley reflected on Muir's actions – on how the sense of reverence gives rise to the deep sense of gratitude and an appreciation of things that are given – in the Article "Generation Wii...or Generation We". Here Muir was fuelled by the awe experienced in the wilderness but Dacher's own work. His own research and work on emotion, particularly the prosocial emotions, inspired him to found the Greater Good Science Centre. Professor Keltner's work as founding director is itself an example of awe in action - the moral elevation and inspiration of his research on Awe spurred his life purpose and drive to help others.

When the attribution of peak experiences come from realising our own best selves and the potential in others, we become a more purposeful and better reasoned agent of change for the common good. There is nothing new about this idea – In his Nicomachean Ethics, Aristotle described the idea of *eudaemonic happiness*, which said, essentially, that happiness was not merely a feeling, or an end goal, but a practice. Aristotle saw happiness not just as a mere state to be enjoyed - but as a goal, and a result from a life well lived - active, engaged and purposeful. It is through service we will come to know the difference between the good life and that of a beautiful life. We should be nurturing the prosocial-emotions, particularly in attempting to ignite that which brings us to action – (for others, the environment and ourselves). "Stop hoping for happiness tomorrow. Happiness is being engaged in the process". [5]

© 2014 THE OUTWARD BOUND TRUST

"The purpose of life education is to encourage students to discover their unique meaning/value of life in order to achieve a state of communal connectedness, personal fulfilment and flourishing, and social responsibility to others, the society, nature, and the universe."

Chang (2016) [6]

AWE ELICITING EXPERIENCES

Think of those times when you were surprised in a way that challenged your comfortable mental structures, when you perhaps found yourselves in some resulting confusion or disorientation - this too is a symptom of the awesome. In this way the emotional response of being in awe may leads us to become a wiser, more enlightened person[7]. In other words, awe can occur when facing a stimulus that is unaccounted for by current knowledge. Awe can transform people and re-orientate their lives, their goals and values. Given the stability of personality and values, awe inducing events may be one of the fastest and most powerful methods of personal change and growth.[8]

Broadly speaking we can say that Awe is elicited by physical, cognitive and interpersonal experiences   Examples of some physical experiences could be accomplishing challenging feats, witnessing the mastery of others, working beyond one's own expectations, witnessing outstanding beauty. We can also feel awe when reliving a memory, reading a brief story or even watching a sixty second commercial. A small dose of awe can give participants a momentary boost in life satisfaction[9].

In a review of the theoretical literature on awe, Dacher Keltner and Jonathan Haidt[10], proposed that awe-eliciting stimuli are characterised by two features: *perceptual vastness* and need for *accommodation*. Although the term "vastness" implies great physical size, in this usage "vast" describes any stimulus that challenges one's accustomed frame of reference in some dimension. A stimulus may convey vastness in physical space, in time, in number, in complexity of detail, in ability, even in volume of human experience. Vastness may be implied by a stimulus, rather than physically inherent in the stimulus. For example, one may experience a sense of vastness in a mathematical equation, not because the equation is literally long, but because of the vast number of observed physical processes it is able to explain and predict. Be it the pleasure of solving a problem, the teamwork in rowing a boat or the feeling of accomplishment on reaching a summit, experiences of awe stand "in the upper reaches of pleasure". Through outdoor adventure or pursuit of studies, this positive emotion of Awe may support significant and lasting change. Through the emotion of awe, we may find a rescaling of our concerns, transcendence of our differences and in sharing our good fortune of being alive we will come to know the feeling that we all humbly share - the bond of *human compassion*.

The positive experience of awe offers us a significant enhancement for learning. Its power lies with its affect of turning us outwards, away from our self concerns whilst helping us appreciate the potential in life with new insights. Through the emotional response and in sensing the vastness, we have need to accommodate such experiences by challenging our existing world view.

In her book *The Human Condition*, Hannah Arendt argues for an appreciation of intrinsic potential in each individual and our need for meaning. Her key concern was that everyone is accountable for their decisions, and yet we may be de-humanised through banality of meaningless labour. Her influential argument supports the power of respecting the potential of human life – specifically with what she calls the natality and plurality of life, i.e. the creation of something new and individual in every person. To Arendt, what is most interesting about an act is not the act itself but the agent it reveals. That we live together not merely for emotional or material support, but also for the pleasure of seeing others reveal their best character.

This here is the impact that authentic Outdoor Adventurous Learning offers children and teachers alike that is so often missed in the many anecdotes. Through outdoor adventure we have means to address banality and purposelessness in life - in recognising we are more than a job holder or consumer, the greatness of the mountains, rivers and lakes become a gift that keeps on giving. Elevated beyond the everyday, beyond the banality of work (and the tendency to devalue one's personal action) we are situated as a free, aware, deciding person. We become part of the aesthetic beauty of that place. As we communicate, use language and make decisions we reveal our differences. It is in this disclosure that we show ourselves to one another in a new light. Through enduring the journey and in sharing its challenges we may find the highest revelation of a person in which we might class as moments of enlightenment or perhaps "glory". The consequences of this are many; With the empowerment effect of elevation and the meaning making of awe, our students find that people do amazing things that often they do not wholly expect. Rather than being captive to their circumstances student's may gain experiences where they have been agents of change. That they can act to change their world and act to be their best self. This is the magic in awe – it can be done as it happens every day in big wilderness settings.

With awe in action we find humanist values emerging experientially. A receptiveness and a will to care emerges that may bind us in harmony and purpose without stultifying human intuition, care and nurture, freedom and inspiration.

A CATALYST FOR CARING

"I regard it as the foremost task of education to insure the survival of these qualities: an enterprising curiosity, an undefeatable spirit, tenacity in pursuit, readiness for sensible self-denial, and above all, compassion"
Kurt Hahn

The propensity of people to attend to the bad more than the good has been known through the ages. Our mammalian brain developed systems out of necessity that would quickly sense danger and allow us to respond. Social neuroscientist, John Cacioppo demonstrated that the brain reacts more strongly to stimuli it deems negative. There is a greater surge in electrical activity.[11] Thus, our attitudes are more heavily influenced by bad rather than good news. This feature of memory which leads people to be more attuned to the bad is generally referred to as negativity bias.[12] As Shakespeare wrote, "the evil that men do lives after them; the good is oft interred with their bones." — Julius Caesar. Not only are we more attuned to negativity, the memory lasts longer too.

Despite this bias, people also have an ancient inherent capacity to be moved and even transformed through positive emotions. This is evident when encountering profound, beautiful or meaningful experiences. A sense of awe can be elicited through witnessing great feats or natural vistas of outstanding scale and beauty or simply through the telling of a story. We may feel its effect on our body as we are in concert

19

with others or lose ourselves to the music or theatre we are observing. In all these examples, we can sense something bigger than our-self which turns us outwards away from our small concerns. The response invoked by the emotions of elevation, awe, admiration and gratitude act as moral amplifiers. They are catalysts for caring.

Various research studies have shown that inducing a sense of awe in people can promote altruistic, helpful and positive social behaviour. Even recalling the memory of an awesome moment made people act more ethically.

The emotion of awe is viewed as part of a set of "self-transcendent" emotions, along with compassion, admiration, elevation and gratitude. Awe may thus be an adaptive part of our fundamentally social nature. Awe takes us outside ourselves by perceiving another authors hand in what we experience. Recent research led by Piercarlo Valdesolo suggests some direct functional outcomes caused by feeling awe. Specifically, awe temporarily reduces peoples tolerance for uncertainty, and this in turn increases their perceptions of external agency (or agency detection) drawing out selflessness. Earlier examples of experimentation, such as those by Keltner, Haidt, Shiota, Schneider, Rudd, Vohs and Piff[13] demonstrate that those who experienced awe and wonder benefitted from positive social behaviours, perspectives, priorities, health and relationship behaviours.

Taking people outside into nature also showed beneficial outcomes. Participants who were asked to stare for one minute at a grove of 200-feet-high blue gum eucalyptus trees were shown to be significantly more helpful. In one simple experiment, a researcher carrying out the follow-up questionnaire staged an accident, pretending to drop a box of pens. According to Piff, the subjects who had stared at the trees picked up significantly more pens. They weren't just more helpful helpers; the awed participants also wanted to be paid half as much for their participation in the study.

When individuals witness others acting compassionately, altruistically or selflessly, their typical reaction of appreciation and admiration is naturally accompanied with warm, open feelings in the chest.[14] People are often profoundly moved by the virtue or skill of others, yet up until recently psychology has not looked that closely at this 'other-praising' family of emotions. Emotions such as elevation, gratitude, and admiration differ from more commonly studied forms of positive affect (joy and amusement) in many ways. The moral emotions mediate between our appraisal and motivation.

- *elevation* (is a response to moral excellence) and motivates prosocial and affiliative behaviour,
- *gratitude* motivates improved relationships with benefactors, and
- *admiration* motivates self-improvement.

Acts of extraordinary moral goodness elicit a distinctive feeling of warmth and expansion that is accompanied by admiration, affection, and even love for the person whose exemplary behaviour is being observed.[15] Psychologists have described the experience of being affected by such acts as a state of **moral elevation**.[16] Jonathan Haidt at Stanford University, considers moral elevation to be closely related to

Awe (in contrast with the opposite emotion of disgust). Moral elevation produces physical changes in the person,[17] is a conscious experience, and motivates a certain type of action tendency,[18] like the wish to emulate the moral exemplar and to act pro-socially. Moral elevation has been likened to the aesthetic experience felt when one beholds a beautiful object or scene. But unlike purely aesthetic experiences, moral elevation can sometimes lead to behavioural changes, eliciting action tendencies associated with the desire to draw closer to other people and to show greater social responsiveness to the needs and interests of others.[19] Notably, this orientation characterizes what ethicists have described as the defining feature of morality.[20]

Elevation elicited by virtuous actions or moral beauty motivates people to behave more virtuously themselves. In addition, observing morally virtuous behaviours often results in individuals feeling optimistic about humanity and creates an enhanced desire to improve; to become our best selves.

As well as the importance of good role models consider the importance of experiencing our own personal example. In good deeds we can be similarly moved just as we would be witnessing another's. We create our own purpose and meaning through our actions. As active participants in the generation of meaning, our interactions with each other and our environment constitute our perception, feeling, thinking as well as our doing. Our action is embodied in the world. We enact the world we live in.

Through moral elevation, we are drawn to become more caring. A study done at the University of Cambridge shows that elevation leads to an increase in altruism. In the study, individuals experiencing elevation were more likely to volunteer to participate in an unpaid study, and spent twice as long helping an experimenter perform tedious tasks compared to those experiencing mirth or in a neutral emotional state. The researchers concluded that witnessing another person's altruistic behaviour elicits elevation, which leads to tangible increases in altruism. According to these results, the best method of encouraging altruistic behaviour may be simply to lead by example.[21]

"By doing good we become good." - Rousseau[22]

Haidt offers an "inspire and rewire" hypothesis to describe momentary experiences that can cause permanent moral transformation. He suggests that powerful moments of elevation may act as a "mental reset button" by erasing cynical or pessimistic feelings and substituting them with feelings of hope, love, and a sensation of moral inspiration.[23] When elevated through example we have the capacity to re-create ourselves, our purpose and others.

The word compassion is itself a verb – it is an action. Many studies have shown Compassion to make people want to help, comfort, or otherwise alleviate the suffering of others.[24] Compassion has a strong tendency to inspire direct pro-social action[25].

The German educator, Kurt Hahn, clearly saw this connection. Hahn's emphasis on the importance of service and the importance he placed on stories such as the Good

Samaritan set an example of such moral elevation in education. Though perhaps Hahn was motivated more by the fact that he himself lived through times where otherwise good people did not raise a hand to help, a time when Jewish people were being openly persecuted. He left Germany in 1938 as an asylum seeker at the outset of World War Two.

An important example of the shame that comes from inaction is the Bystander Phenomenon. It was first demonstrated in the laboratory by John M. Darley and Latané in 1968 after they became interested in the topic following a murder in 1964 in which people failed to rescue (Kitty Genovese was brutally attacked and over thirty witnesses did not intervene to help her, each feeling that someone else would do so). The researchers launched a series of experiments that resulted in one of the strongest and most replicable effects in social psychology. Darley's study on the "bystander effect" – revealed the processes that influence how and when we help people. How the sense of personal responsibility was diluted by an increased number of onlookers. We can draw uncomfortable parallels from history when the inaction of people led to much suffering and injustice on an inconceivable scale. The story of the Biafra Airlift is an example of compassion in action - when a band of people refuse to be bystanders and, acting on a higher conscience, railed against the officials and authorities. Their courage and action saved one million children.[26]

Here's the tricky part. In our daily lives, the disproportionate weight of the negativity bias suggests that our need for moral elevation and instances of awe cannot just be merely assigned to peak moments. Occasional big positive experiences don't necessarily make sufficient impact on our brain to override the tilt to negative scepticism. We need small and frequent positive experiences to help tip the scales. Through looking at relationships, researchers[27] have shown that this is more than a matter of a fifty-fifty balance. They found a specific ratio exists between the amount of positivity and negativity required to account for our negativity bias. That ratio is five to one. As long as there was five times as much positive feeling and positive interaction as there was negative, we would counter the negativity effect. This then asks more of us than to be passive recipients. The best way to encounter catalysts such as awe, admiration and elevation was to be creators of these emotions- in action. Through our deeds and openness, we can become each other's best catalyst for compassion.

A Hopi Elder Speaks...

You have been telling the people that this is the Eleventh Hour.
Now you must go back and tell the people that this IS the hour
and there are things to be considered...
Where are you living? What are you doing?
What are your relationships? Are you in right relation?
Where is your water? Know your garden.
It is time to speak your truth, create your community, be good
to each other. And do not look outside yourself for the leader.
This could be a good time!
There is a river flowing now very fast. It is so great and swift,
that there are those who will be afraid. Know the river has its
destination. The elders say we must let go of the shore — push
off into the middle of the river, keep our eyes open, and our
heads above the water. See who is in there with you and
celebrate.
At this time in history, we are to take nothing personally, least
of all, ourselves. For when we do, our spiritual growth and
journey comes to a halt.
The time of the lone wolf is over. Gather yourselves;
Banish the word "struggle" from your attitude and your
vocabulary. All that we do now must be done in a sacred
manner and in celebration.
We are the ones we have been waiting for!

Tribute credited to Hopi Chief Dan Evehema, who passed away
in 1999 aged 106. © Manataka American Indian Council.
www.manataka.org

What We Can Learn From Ten Year Old's

"Children are not the people of tomorrow, but people today. They are entitled to be taken seriously…They should be allowed to grow into whoever they were meant to be - The unknown person inside each of them is the hope for the future" - Januez Korzack

"How wonderful it is that nobody need wait a single moment before starting to improve the world"– Anne Frank

Januez Korzack was an innovator of the educational system, not as well-known as others, but he was the first to reach the conclusion and to act for his belief that a child has the same rights as the adult. He believed that within each child there burned a moral spark that could vanquish the darkness at the core of human nature. To prevent that spark from being extinguished, one had to love and nurture the young, make it possible for them to believe in truth and justice. Korczak had always stressed the importance of 'listening to and learning from children'. He saw the child not as a creature who needs help, but as a person in their own right.

Children can show us how to be better. Children show adults what integration and compassion can look like. The ten-year olds of one Birmingham Primary School did this through their example and actions. In 2016 this primary school was designated to have an increased intake of children to create a new form entry, in effect a third class. The school's catchment was a comfortable leafy suburban neighbourhood and parents were involved with the school and cared greatly about their children. However, when the parents found that the new children were from immigrant families whose faith and needs were so different and possibly demanding, it caused great anxiety and consternation amongst parents. The parent's conservative and protective nature was not helped by grapevine mutterings. In confronting the school, the parents asked that the new children be set into a separate new classroom, so their needs wouldn't adversely affect their own. However, at the point when classes were to be re-shuffled, their children refused and through holding hands with their new classmates they demonstrated they that they are all friends and will be together. Together in action the children made this message of respect clear to their parents and school. Listening to their children the parents were both humbled and elevated.

Tolstoy wrote of such similar instances of wisdom in his stories and fables.[28] For him the moral law is present in the hearts of everyone. It is so simple that it is readily understood by children, even if it is often ignored by adults. His favourite quote was from Matthew 1.1.25. *"You have hidden these things from the wise and the intelligent and revealed them to infants"*

Look to the gifts from children in making for a very successful school community. In the primary years they still have the openness to share their awe prone outlook and enthusiasm with older students. We may have a young leaders programme that allows students to mentor their younger primary peers- consider the opportunity for the mentoring to go both ways. To keep the sparks of enthusiasm burning in our adolescent's daily lives, be mindful of how younger children can remind them how to experience wonder, fun and the wisdom in honesty and humility. Children remain present in the now; they open all their senses to what they're experiencing; and they engage their hearts — not just their minds — as they experience and reflect on the world around them. Children have the most valuable lessons for us if we listen.

THE HUMAN CONDITION –
TIES TO EACH OTHER

"Less and less is life animated through personal discovery, intimacy with others, or self-reflection. While life has become more manageable for many people, it has become commensurately less engaged" Kirk Schneider

It's a startling fact to consider that we have far more in common with others around us than we do with our younger selves of ten or fifteen years ago. We are motivated to find our place in our families, at school, at work and in society. *The human condition is socially embedded,* and we are necessarily political and social - bound by our need to belong to each other.

Humans have had to adapt socially and culturally for their survival over the ages - sustaining a web of human relationships through social interaction was essential. Society came to be for the sake of life and exists for the sake of the good life (Aristotle again!). In relating to the world, our human condition relates to each of these social needs:

1)   to feel CONNECTED- to belong, to fit in, to feel secure,

2)   to feel CAPABLE - competent and to take responsibility,
3)   to feel we COUNT - that we make a difference or to feel
      significant; and
4)   to feel COURAGE - to be able to handle difficult
      situations and overcome our fears.

These have been referred to as the four "*Crucial Cs*" (Bettner & Lew, 1990) and represent our fundamental psychological needs in any group. As goals they form an individual's characteristic ways of feeling and behaving (or misbehaving) in groups.

> "*When we feel we cannot connect, we are likely to engage in attention seeking; when we do not feel capable, we are likely to make bids for power; when we do not feel we count, we may seek revenge and hurt others the way we've been hurt; when we lose courage, we assume disability and seek to avoid life's demands.*" (John, K: 2011)

With the most disengaged there is the need for getting to "the right place". To do so needs a healing journey to address through rediscovering that which binds us all:

- Who am I? My relationship with self and others.
- Where is my Place? - My relationship with the world
- What is my Purpose? - The relationship with myself.

Through action the lives of each of us gains a significance. Indeed, something great happens when an individual begins to see social action of interest to their own welfare –that in helping others they are helping themselves.

Just as we will argue for the embodied mind – that body and brain are not separate- we must see that the same must hold for mind and society, for a person and their world are inseparable. Ours is a social brain and our human nature, rather than being fixed or innate, evolves in step with our cultural capacities.

"To define human nature ...would be like "jumping over one's own shadow" Hannah Arendt 1958

We must instead look to the Human Condition: *"The impact of the world's reality upon human existence is felt and received as a conditioning force. Whatever touches or enters into a sustained relationship with human life immediately assumes the character of a condition of human existence. This is why, no matter what we do, we are always conditioned beings.[29]"* We are active participants in the generation of life's meaning and purpose. What we experience is itself shaped by our own actions.

Through our deeds and words, we are continually answering the question asked of us "Who are you?" Each of us is capable of new perspectives and new actions. We have the capacity to recreate and renew again and again.

The ancient Greeks saw action as the supreme blessing of human life. We underestimate ourselves when we confuse self with the narrow ego. We "see ourselves in others". The joy and meaning of life is increased through the fulfilment of each person's potential together.[30] Collaborating and cooperating with one another as individuals and communities' benefits society more than we can know. We should never underestimate that potential which springs up between people when people act "in concert" for the greater good. Action has boundless consequences, often going far beyond what we could anticipate.

EMOTION & THE NEED FOR PURPOSE

"Hunger not to have, hunger to be" J. Dewey

"Now no feeling can be relied on to last in its full intensity, or even last at all. Knowledge can last, habits can last, but feelings come & go." -C.S. Lewis

Such a fleeting thing is an emotion. It lasts but for a few seconds, igniting as a subconscious spark that can evoke the deepest of physiological reactions. Emotions evolved for their adaptive value in dealing with fundamental life-tasks. There are universal predicaments such as achievements, losses, frustrations, etc.[31] Thus we often experience emotions as happening to us, not chosen by us.

Emotions are undoubtedly strong and very capable of bringing out the best and worst in us. It is said all emotion either rewards or punishes. And whilst we can find ourselves overwhelmed by feelings, they come and go. Knowledge, principles, and habits are seen as the enduring qualities that make you, you. Yet new understanding shows us how emotion can have a greater role in defining *who we can be*.

In the original behaviourist model of emotion, it was argued that emotions are not chosen, but evoked as a conditioned response to stimuli (Watson, 1924). An automatic involuntary aspect is present in the experience of all emotion.[32] As emotion results in some part from an automatic appraisal there will be some conditioning within to control what is

33

happening. One can't simply elect when to have which emotion- it occurs before conscious choice. However, when there is a reason or an incentive, that appraisal is conditioned in line with one's purpose. Recent work challenges the classical behaviourist view. Emotions are widely recognized to be motivating.[33] In fact the word "emotion" comes from the same Latin root as *movere,* the verb to move.

When emotions are the product of extended appraisal and the onset is more gradual it is more possible to influence what feeling one is beginning to experience. Emotions show signs of being goal-directed. That is, they are at least partially in the realm of reward-governed behaviours, not conditioned responses; they are selected by their consequences, not their antecedents.

Emotion is still a reflex but it is ultimately *pulled by incentives rather than pushed by stimuli.* This is important - What is your goal? What is your purpose?   Through meaning we begin to have a choice, in our emotional life we begin to unlock potential previously unknown to the self.

In his book, *The Path to Purpose,* William Damon wrote of the immediate benefits from having purpose: In a series of studies of over 1,200 youth, aged 12 to 26, Damon found that those who were actively pursuing a clear purpose, reaped tremendous benefits that were both immediate and that could also last a lifetime. Benefits such as an extra positive energy that not only kept students motivated to pursue their purpose, making them very strong learners, but opened them to positive emotions such as gratitude, self-confidence, optimism and a deep sense of fulfilment.

Today's students may be high achievers but scratch the surface; you might find many will have no idea what for. This sense of meaninglessness is one of the main contributors to the high depression rates among our youth. Young people, in fact all of us, benefit from having a purpose in life - something meaningful to ourselves that also serves the "greater good".

The world we inhabit is manufactured of 'meaning' rather than 'information'. We are adept meaning makers thinking in metaphor and resting on our own shifting context. The reality in which we find ourselves, is a world itself brought forth by our ways of communicating and our joint action. A seemingly natural experience is thoroughly intertwined with sociocultural realities.[34]

The moral emotions then affect us according to how we see the world - our map of reality and how we enaction our lives.[35] Thus, the enduring qualities of knowledge, principles, and habits are aligned with our motivations and our purpose – the reasons why we become who we are.

"You cannot stay on the summit forever, you have to come down again. So why bother in the first place?

Just this: What is above knows what is below, but what is below does not know what is above. One climbs, one sees. One descends, one sees no longer, but one has seen" - Rene Daumal

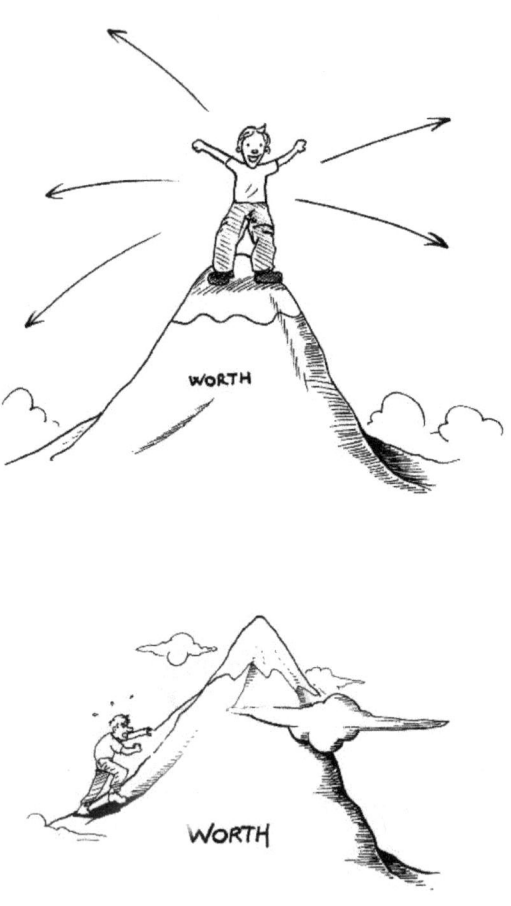

COMPLEXITY THEORY AND BREAK THROUGHS

"Human resources are like natural resources; they're often buried deep. You have to go looking for them, they're not just lying around on the surface. You have to create the circumstances where they show themselves." —Sir Ken Robinson

The complex learning environment of outdoor adventurous learning is a key reason it is successful for developing young people. The combination of challenge, social processes and situation mean that outdoor adventurous experiences provide exceptional opportunities for the development of social and emotional skills. Whether it results in experiencing the flow of performance or a new-found vision of personal potential, a rejuvenated source of inner worth arises. The potential for transformational change to occur through high impact outdoor education is clear, yet typically education research only provides anecdotal case studies or self-reporting data, prone to bias, as evidence. In a PhD thesis by Randall Williams "The Impact of Residential Adventure Education on Primary School Pupils" the argument for evaluated educational outcomes based on linear assumptions was neatly dissected.[36] Randall suggested complexity theory as a more viable approach to understanding the great impact that Outdoor Adventurous Learning offers:

"For many young people, a school journey will be their only experience of life outside the city. They may never have seen the stars

unimpeded by the glare of sodium lights...Yet, without first hand awareness of the natural world, how can we expect our children to rise to the challenge of being responsible custodians of the planet? Children need to experience the world outside the city. Nature needs children....In terms of self-aware autonomy, children often discover their real abilities for the first time and develop enhanced self- [knowledge] confidence and independence. In terms of capacity for empathy, living and working closely with others opens their eyes to an understanding of other people and how to relate effectively to one another... Many children discover for the first time that they can succeed, a discovery that has a direct effect on their subsequent engagement and motivation. However, opportunity is far from equal, particularly for those who need it most... [There is need to] grasp the nettle of embedding such experiences in the curriculum and making them an expectation for all young people. To do so would address the current inequality and allow all young people to access what is both an important part of their heritage and a powerful educational experience." Williams (2011)

Human nature is complex, beliefs are self-reinforcing and situations more random that we would wish. At the right moment an interaction or a new situation may result in an experience that brings great personal insight and change. Life's turning points are like this. The wise teacher knows too well that learning is not a simple linear input-output function. We must put a lot of work in to building foundations – for some children it may seem that they will never progress, and then, suddenly, a blossoming occurs.[37] With the right circumstances and experiences students can gain insights that markedly change their behaviour. How they were yesterday does not necessarily mean how they will be tomorrow. The nature of being awestruck by vastness, elevated through excellence (or spirit from completing something of deep personal value), present opportunities to make such paradigm shifts happen. Thus it is of the utmost importance that an adult maintains their belief in a child - to keep the door open- so as not to preclude the opportunity for such a leap to occur. In this way it is essential that opportunities are made for children to experience inspiring places, big geographies, beautiful nature and excellent performances that elevate them from their daily routine.

The peak experience known as Flow is a good example of how positive learning behaviours can arise suddenly.[38] Flow arises when our actions and awareness merge such that the situation results in the sudden overwhelming enjoyment and loss of self in our work. Flow is a non-linear occurrence predicted by the balance between perceived challenge, personal competence and the right opportunity for action.

Just as with Flow, the transformational impact of awe and moral elevation are situated, highly personal and temporal. The high state of Flow has the potential for raising self-worth, aspiration and self-perception. *Similarly, in experiencing occasions of awe, and moral elevation we have a non-linear model that can help us to better understand how the potential of situations and emotions work to support transformational breakthroughs in behaviours and relationships.*

Complexity Theory is a non-linear approach which has been powerful in modelling instances of sudden dynamic changes. To understand, consider the analogy of a bridge suddenly collapsing after being incrementally laden with weight. Bit by bit the bridge gradually bends and that can be represented by a direct relationship between the weight added and the degree of deformity that our linear thinking brains can accept. Up until a point that is! – until one gram extra is added and the whole structure collapses! This is the "Catastrophe" that the simple relationship between load and bending did not predict! Its collapse is a non-linear event. The model known as the **cusp catastrophe model** represents moments of non-linear "leaps" or a jump to another relationship.

Figure 9 represents a model for the occurrence of Flow-state, depicts a non-linear "leap", moving from the lower plane of behaviours to the upper surface with higher levels of enjoyment, interest and intrinsic motivation. The new behaviours occur spontaneously and automatically simply as a result of the complex interactions within the system, rather than in response to specific causal factors (Haggis, 2008). I would suggest the affect of Awe too works like this. We can all jump up to a new plane of possible behaviours just as we can fall back from them. In this way such a model maps both the continuous and abrupt changes in the behaviours we see in our students over time.

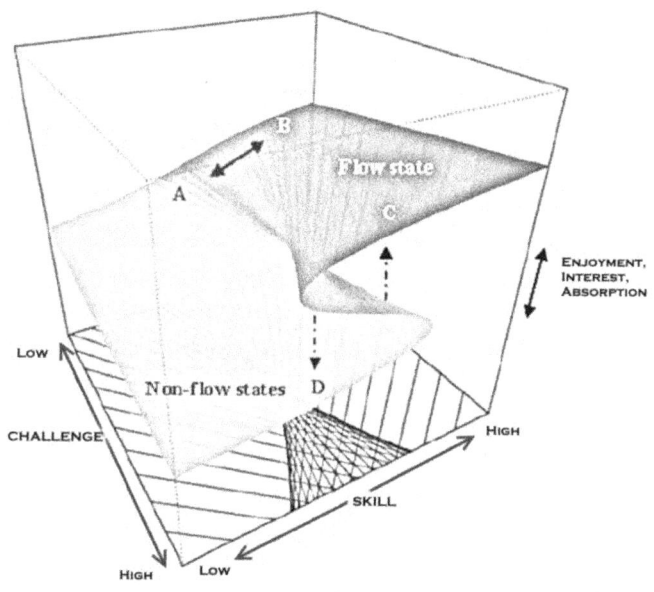

Figure 2: Graph of a Cusp Catastrophe Model for Flow

Complexity and non-linearity has a number of implications for us as educators. First, it implies that the behaviour of the whole cannot be reduced to the sum of its parts. Second, it guarantees that small changes can have large results. Third, it opens up the potential for transformative change[39]. No doubt, many educators have found each of these implications through their work and consequently are far more understanding of the needs for a child's emerging identity.

VIRTUES IN ACTION

'...to become attached to society, the child must feel in it something that is real, alive and powerful, which dominates the person and to which he owes the best part of himself' – Emile Durkheim.

"The only ones among you who will be truly happy are those who have sought and found how to serve." Albert Schweitzer

Welcoming, respectful, organised, generous, confident and proud... is that the impression one gets when entering your school's door? These qualities tell a story... not just to you as the visitor but to the children and their teachers each day. They are the communities' values made explicit. How do pupils move around the school? What levels of respect and ownership are felt by all. *The sense of belonging.* Speak of this to those embattled teachers and they, lost in delivery and surviving "in the trenches", may look at you in despair. In the poorest of communities come the poorest of schools. Our teachers need to be supported, the school needs to set clear boundaries and protect them. Children in our most socially disadvantaged communities need their teachers for somebody to look up to... and yet their teachers are overworked, stressed, under-appreciated and unhappy. Who is flourishing in the life of these children... *Anyone?*

Where do you start with a struggling school culture? One can't easily restart from scratch. So many books are written about this alone. It has become a business. There are many off-the-shelf offers marketed as solutions, fixes and easily implemented strategies... yet despite all this the crux has still to be over-come. The crux is the community.

The pursuit of excellence in all matters overlooks the fact that life is complex and often messy. Looking at personal qualities alone fails to discriminate between what is important and what is not... that practical wisdom emerges itself from the very complexity of life. In the single pursuit of personal performance and attainment, too many of our children grow up without the feeling of being good for anything to themselves or others.

A person's character qualities are not developed in isolation. At the heart of the virtue approach to ethics is the idea of "community". We develop within and by the communities to which we belong (Velasquez, Andre, et al :1988). In challenging the status-quo we begin to find wisdom and solutions to the problems of our poorest communities, principally those arising from alienation, inequity and powerlessness. It is through attending to meaning in the lives of our children and active engagement we support the development of character within our communities, the children and ourselves.

Focusing on intellectual virtues and performance alone is not a sustainable approach for supporting good qualities of character. Indeed, the lack of moderation and single-minded pursuit of academic attainment is damaging to children's wellbeing and spirit. There must be a balance of endeavour to be successful.

Figure 3: A Framework for Character Development

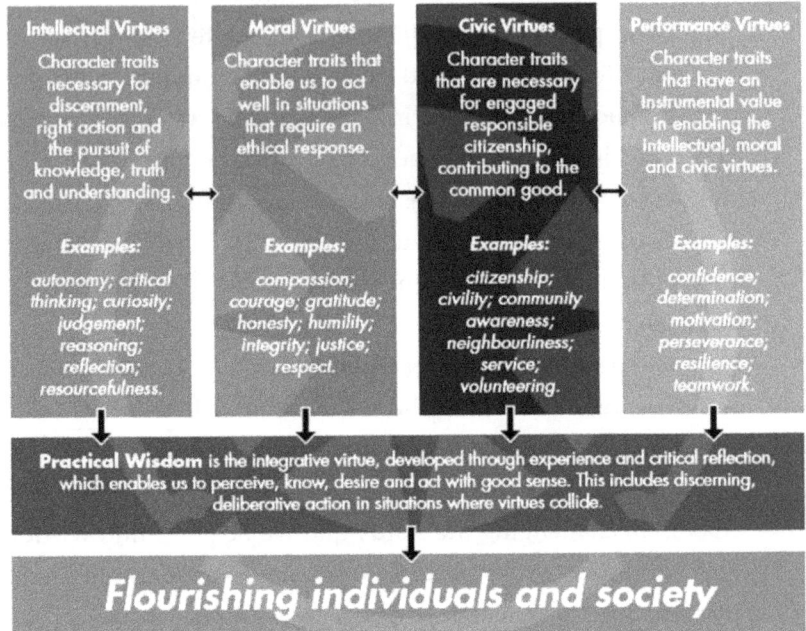

© Jubilee Centre for Character & Virtue.

There is a clear need to address both moral and civic virtues in education. The Jubilee Centre for Character and Virtue presents a framework depicted in Figure-1 that provides for more balance in the approach to developing character. Knowing what the best course of action to do in different life circumstances requires practical wisdom. Providing for a broad range of experiences allows our children to grow in their practical wisdom (known as *Phronesis*). Through experiential learning we provide space for our children to not only see qualities and virtues in themselves, but also to care about doing them.

The roots of change reach into the community. To turn a learning culture around we must provide for connections that were not there before - we must offer hope. We cannot successfully educate in isolation to the contours of our communities and the habits of character they encourage and instil.[40] Engaging the community with the school takes time and courage. Each school is as individual as a person. The school leader who looks beyond the gates will see the contours. Their tenacity of spirit and strong hand may steer the course if the right connections are made. The cultural emergence of a successful school is a wonderful accomplishment for any community. Hope starts to be made material. Empathy and wisdom is evident and captures the hearts and minds of staff and students alike. Standards are normalised as the relationships transform to become orderly, respectful, trustful and ultimately productive. Character, rather than being a list of words is the visible behaviours, values and relationships in action.

To assist, lets offer the ethic of service and opportunities for compassion to help steer our youth.

The starting point? One can feel it as you walk into a school. Visit many schools and you will grow a sense for the culture. Beyond words, there is no replacement for a strong engaged leadership team – for sharing a clear vision and belief. The leader must have Charisma, Ethos and be about Action.

Let's move away from clever acronyms and soundbites, those long lists of aims and character qualities on the school web page and look at our children as they are - not as we would imagine them to be. It is their school and their call to action. Without any living practice to substantiate the vision; without the opportunities and skills to enable children to express and practice virtues we have a hollow offering.

Our children are not emotionally inert. They read the culture fluently and it tells them something about themselves. It is well known by psychologists that we use our own behaviour as a guide to help us determine our own thoughts and feelings.[41] We are all susceptible to the influence of environment. Our children are especially vulnerable to the social situation. A positive culture gives cause for positive behaviours – and vice versa.

"The best practice is where teachers have the nerve to break away from thinking that learning is about four sessions where the curtain goes up and you are on stage trying to entertain and educate children."[42] *Professor Mick Waters*

Our children and teachers are socialised by the system. It is up to us to facilitate the opportunities that develop cultures of practice with virtues that are shared and lived by all. Professor Waters speaks about the need for courage in learning, teaching and leadership in this regard as ways to reclaim "the system" for the profession and our children. He refers us to a traditional Native American model called *"The Circle of Courage"* that highlights the interconnection between values of proficiency, autonomy, belonging and generosity. The model is formalised by Professor Larry Brendtro's work from over two decades of practice with children and youth at risk.[43] It proposes that, with courage, we can move to a more compassionate and respectful environment where virtuous behaviour builds with personal effort.

When lost in delivery, both teacher and student will not know how to be any different. To this end lets respect the need to provide opportunities for giving and service for our children so they will develop a sense of civility. Behaviour becomes our character, through our choices – lets open up possibilities. For the good we do makes us good. Let's provide experiences for justice, compassion and gratitude - engaging our students with something greater than themselves so they will understand the importance of humility and wisdom. That they will enjoy the fulfilment from service and not underestimate the power of their moral voice.

By impelling our children into awe inducing experiences, by giving them voice and cause for social action, our students will discover what they can be. They will grow to discover virtues for their needs, - not so much as a creation of the school, but an emergence from school. From their contribution emerges self-worth, from self-worth arises the aspiration to be ones best self. Through this spirit they may know of their own virtuous potential and flourish in harmony with others.

Our modern culture overwhelms us with individualism. But can we experience a flourishing human life without influence from another human? In the essence of Ubuntu, a traditional South African philosophy:

"I am what I am because of who we all are."

47

What was the Moment

What was the moment
when I turned from building
trophies and shallow glories
to selfless actions that made the turn?

What was the moment
when I changed from talk
to doing the small things
that led me closer to myself and the land before me?

What was the moment
when the mountains became
more than playgrounds but
wisdom whispering a wild truth
at first I refused to hear?

When was the day I threw my life into the forest and the mountains,
deep into the oceans and rivers to almost drown in a fight for their salvation
for my own salvation?

Was it because years before I stood in the shade of an ancient tree
and saw a swallow fly through the air lilting low before me and then turn
and touch me with her blue blue-wings?

Was it then?
Or was it the moment
I went into a wild night to escape
only to find after nights alone beneath the sea-sweep of stars
there is no escape
but the courage to return and so turn the tide?

What was the moment when I knew
what needed to be done, or was the knowing always there
waiting for reply?

I find others too now who walk unknown
in a land pathless to the horizon
and know the moment never was a moment
but the only choice once I turned to listen.

- by Galeo Saintz, for Kristine McDivitt Tompkins

PART TWO

SKILLS FOR LIFE

SKILLS FOR LIFE

"We are the product of our practice " Anders Ericsson [44]

"A child is the only known substance from which a responsible adult can be made" Thomas Likona

Much has been made for addressing the quantity of content in education in recent years. The Core Knowledge (CK) approach of Professor E.D. Hirsch seeks to readdress educational inequalities—many of which arise from a failure to understand the things that others take for granted by the transmission of a specific body of knowledge to children over their primary years. Facts that are widely used and taken for granted by competent writers and speakers are taught to develop a sense of cultural literacy. CK is convincing as a necessary foundation for allowing higher-order reading, writing and thinking skills that children need for academic and vocational success *"knowledge does not get in the way of reasoning: it's what we reason with."*

Influential author Eric Kalenze argues that whilst education needs significant reform, most of the current reform movements focus too much on structures, and not enough on content[45]. Supporters of Hirsch's Core Knowledge model such as the brilliant Daisy Christodoulou[46] make strong arguments for the increase of declarative knowledge content in schools – that the memorisation of facts is being neglected in modern education because of the priority given to procedural knowledge such as skills.

Whilst such authors commendably argue for raising levels of achievement irrespective of socio-economic background they argue that learning through discovery is "criminally wasteful". It seems breath-taking that they discard the necessity of positive experiential intervention. The emergence of poor behaviours coincides with negative attitudes to education. The poverty of opportunity in our most deprived communities persists with unemployment and low levels of wellbeing and an absence of aspiration. Not all children come able and ready to absorb the requisite knowledge, nor are all schools able to achieve such tasks without requisite climate and conditioning.

In Anders Ericsson's book on deliberate practice titled, "Peak", he views high performers as not simply domain-specific experts but as experts in maintaining high levels of practice and improving performance. His research highlights the extent to which effort and motivation levels act as a constraint or a gateway to learning and achievement. Deliberate practice is certainly effective in improving performance yet requires a lot of effort and asks for high levels of engagement since deliberate practice is not inherently motivating. There is obviously a lot more to learning than the memorisation of core facts. Attitudes, behaviours and skills are integral to the endeavour. Qualities of character have a role to play, so too does addressing requisite support and encouragement from family.

If we can accept Hirsch's Core Knowledge model, then there is an argument for extending the concept to account for Core Experiences. Many do not have such fundamental experiences from which to grow from. Just as CK addressed that body of knowledge is taken for granted rather than being explained when it is used, we too overlook key experiences.

Declarative knowledge is important, but a level playing field must also recognise the opportunity gap, the social capital gap and the skills gap that exists - and which can be convenient to ignore when using evaluation to propose silver bullet policy recommendations. Not all children come from homes that value education, are loving, or have access to local resources in a city like London or are gifted and recognised and are fortunate to be supported with scholarship onto inspirational education routes.

There is need to factor in the poverty of opportunity prevalent in our most deprived communities. That is opportunities for experiences to provide aesthetic and sensory knowledge as a child would gain from experiencing the seaside, being immersed in nature, seeing stars, a museum or art gallery. Opportunities for positive experiences are necessary and there is much we would take for granted. Learning does not stop when class ends. Even more acutely so when it comes to developing virtues. We do not turn off character education, we are living it.

Through powerful experiences of working together, being immersed in beauty, contributing to good causes and other potential opportunities for being elevated and awe inspired, we offer a powerful means to build positive behaviours, skills and wisdom.

We should never discount the importance of deliberately developing procedural knowledge, as skills and behaviours. There is a crucial need to support our young people in developing personal skills, so they are better able to be resilient, courageous, compassionate, creative and wise in their lives. These qualities are skills for life.

THE IMPACT MENTAL HEALTH ISSUES HAVE ON SCHOOLS

Public Health England (PHE) suggest that in an average class of 30 pupils aged 15

10 ARE LIKELY TO HAVE WITNESSED THEIR PARENTS' SEPARATION

3 OF THEM COULD HAVE A MENTAL DISORDER

7 ARE LIKELY TO HAVE BEEN BULLIED

6 ARE POSSIBLY SELF-HARMING

1 MAY HAVE EXPERIENCED THE DEATH OF A PARENT

Source: Public Health England (2015)

THE PANACEA OF CHARACTER TRAITS
Towards a model for situation-oriented skills

"I learned very early the difference between knowing the name of something and knowing something" Richard Feynman

"In the beginner's mind there are many possibilities, but in the expert's, there are few." Shunryu Suzuki

It is natural that we instinctively look to the personal qualities of an individual to guess their future conduct and behaviour. We will avoid the temperamental and be wary of the dishonest. Over the years, psychologists have been keen on identifying traits that best predict behaviours for economic, development or health reasons. Trait Theory research arose from this, which suggests that the broad personality classification is very stable in adults over time and associated with a range of important life outcomes, such as wellbeing academic and occupational success and marital stability. One of the major models is known as The Big Five personality traits- a model popularly used in recruitment. This model assumes one can map out the dimensions of personality for each of us with a combination of the five characteristics. In turn, the recruiter has a view as to our suitability in employment and success in the job. Such research is done retrospectively looking at qualities that are assumed to be pre-existing and *unchangeable*.

As educators should we not question this level of determinism? To assume we are the same people now as we were when children, but also that our future lives will be predetermined regardless of skills acquisition would seem overly simplistic. The truth has been lost in the averages.

The Big Five Personality Traits
1. Openness,
2. Conscientiousness,
3. Extraversion,
4. Agreeableness, and
5. Neuroticism.

Such models do not inform a parent or teacher on how best to instil the character qualities in their children, nor account for context (such as levels of social capital, socio and economic opportunity, home stability and health). Such factors act as *enabling conditions* and greatly differ between poor and affluent communities. The Trait Theory implicitly assumes these traits are already pre-determined in us and, as such, is vulnerable to political quasi social experiments or convenience for policy rationale. We should be wary of models where the pursuit of classification seems to be the goal rather than an understanding of the causes or consequences of the categorised behaviours.

What use is a set of static and unchangeable traits to the educator? We should be interested in those skills that can be built, wisdom to rely upon to grow ones qualities - the social emotional skills - that which can change trajectories and can bring happiness in relationship and life. Here lies the impact in character education. We should be clear the goals are for change and betterment and be prepared to challenge the panacea of a "character" approach. From the outset one should be vigilant lest they encounter hints of determinism in classification, or discrimination based on immutable traits.

In recent years there has been a revival of interest in Character Traits with hierarchies of strengths being proposed to assist in developing practical applications – mainly by classifying and measuring positive traits.[47] Of great significance is Christopher Peterson and Martin Seligman's book, *Character Strengths and Virtues* which proposes a measure of "humanist ideals" or virtues. They were clear that this measure proved beyond their ability to specify a technical theory and disavowed any intent to offer their work as a taxonomy. Theirs, they argued, was an aspirational classification of strengths and virtues.

They studied all major religions and philosophical traditions and found that the six virtues were shared in practically all cultures throughout history. They proposed six classes of virtues: *Wisdom and Knowledge, Courage, Humanity, Justice, Temperance and Transcendence.*

Since these virtues are so broad they began to focus attention on measuring various character traits which they believe achieved the virtues. Patterson and Seligman proposed a measurement of "good character" based on different kinds of positive traits (called character strengths) i.e. authenticity, persistence, kindness, gratitude, hope, sense of humour, and so on.[48]

Implicitly assumed in this approach is that such character traits would be consistent in predicting behaviour across different situations. But in practice, capturing Character

Traits can suggest too simple a frame which overlooks the complex network connections behind behaviour and personality. Seligman admits their approach is that of Trait Theory but argues for it through the lens of a new psychology that recognises the personal and situational context and capacity for change.[49] However, if it looks like a taxonomy and is used as a form of personal assessment, then it is vulnerable to misuse. There are vested political interests associated with the invariance of Character Traits which argue for the divestment of costly progressive projects for social mobility and disadvantaged communities.

If only people were so straight forward as to be so easily predictable. As individuals, we just don't behave as consistently as such theories or categorisations of character would have us expect. There is a *fundamental attribution error* in our tendency to explain away someone's behaviour based on their personal factors, such as personality or disposition, and to underestimate the degree that external factors, such as situational influences, influence behaviours. Little surprise then that research[50] advises some caution with the trait theories. There are very few circumstances where free will plays little or no role in what we do.

According to research by Mark Snyder, a psychologist at the University of Minnesota, people seem to differ in how much situations affect their actions. In *"Public Appearances, Private Reality"* Dr Snyder reviews evidence showing that some people are virtual chameleons, shaping themselves to blend into whatever social situation they find themselves in, while others are almost oblivious to the special demands and expectations of differing situations, being more or less the same person regardless of where they are. *"It is as though each type were playing to a different audience, one inner, the other outer"* says Dr. Snyder.

The situation-oriented, are skilled at social roles and being adept at different situations. They flourish in jobs where they deal with a range of different groups. Those less affected by situations are more consistent in their behaviour, putting less effort into role-playing: They have a *"smaller wardrobe"*, wearing the same clothes in more situations, than do the situation-oriented. To top it off, studies such as that by Fleeson and Wilt (2010)[51] have shown that the measured traits do not necessarily reflect a person's own self-concept and are inconsistent with an individual's view on their authenticity. Thus, depending on a given situation an introverted person may behave in an extroverted manner and vice versa.[52] An individual's behaviour is not simply an interaction of five permanent character traits but is fundamentally dependent on the needs of a given situation[53]. This is *'arguably, a richer conception of education that considers reason, feeling and emotion'*[54] We should not differentiate between ones' character traits and their virtues. Virtues in action is character.

HOW PERSONAL QUALITIES ARISE THROUGH SITUATIONS

"The experience of helping a fellow man in danger, or even of training in a realistic manner to be ready to give this help, tends to change the balance of power in a youth's inner life with the result that compassion can become the master motive."- Kurt Hahn
"children need not only to be able to tell right from wrong but to care about which is which: in other words, develop virtues " (Haydon, 2006: 63).

Personal qualities arise from our continual interaction with situations whether ordinary or extraordinary. As we have argued, an individual's behaviour is not simply an interaction of five permanent character traits, but is fundamentally, dependent on the needs of a given situation. We are co-authors with the situation.

Heroic and kind actions may arise only when and if the situation does - in other times they may not be apparent to us or others. In reflecting on our qualities, we account for our skill in interacting with the world- the ever-changing situational variables both real and imagined. The development of cognitive skills that help condition our personal development may help us better negotiate the slings and arrows of fortune. In self-awareness the self emerges.

Self-perception through action is an important consideration in behaviour. When we have the chance to act positively we feel good about ourselves. When we feel good we are more likely to think and thus act in a positive manner again. The thoughts, actions and feelings we have can feed each other as a virtuous cycle (or, if negative, a vicious circle).

The impact of this circular relationship was successfully seen in a school-based social-emotional and character development programme called *"Positive Action."*[55] Research by Brian Flay and colleagues in 2013 on Hawaiian schools demonstrated how the use of a social- emotional and character development intervention can improve academic outcomes.[56] In this intervention, students learn the Thoughts-Actions-Feelings about Self Circle. (A circular model depicts how thoughts lead to actions and actions to feelings about the self, which lead to more thoughts). When this cycle is negative, students did not want to learn. The essence of the program is to emphasize those actions that promote a healthy and positive cycle were students will want to learn. This study robustly demonstrated that supporting children's skills and knowledge relating to their social emotional behaviours can improve their motivation, engagement with learning and qualities of behaviour.

"every experience lives on in further experiences." (Dewey:1938)

Our way of being and interaction with our situation is greatly influenced by our level of skill and experience. One of the best examples of this is the work of Walter Mischel who was the creator of one of the most famous experiments in the history of psychology - he devised the "marshmallow test" whose results have since demonstrated the importance of self-control in life outcomes.[57] The study showed that the longer a child was able to wait the better they would fare later in life at numerous measures of what we now call *executive function*. Dr Mischel travelled around the world and despite various cultural and socioeconomic contexts, the results on delayed gratification seemed universal. Some children seemed to have a greater ability to self-control than others. This might have all led to a reaffirmation to the Traits Model, but for Mischel's finding that a person's executive function, (their ability for self-control), is just another learnable skill. Like a muscle, the more you use it, the stronger it gets.[58] The skills which enable us to delay gratification are the same skills that allow us to make other good choices - a way to really improve human choice and freedom.

Mischel also wrote an influential article in 1968 arguing that circumstances can be more powerful than traits when predicting the behaviour of a person. Specifically, that the variation in expression of a given trait from situation to situation is so great that the notion of personality traits itself was of limited use in accounting for how people behave. In comparison, the personality view claims that behaviour depends on a person's long-term personality traits and these manifested in whatever circumstance a person is immersed in. Yet *"Any trait can vary with the moment"*, Mischel found through experimentation that behaviour arises through an ongoing dialogue between self and situation. That distinctive but stable patterns of "if-then" situation-behaviour relations occur.

Mischel wanted these if-then contingencies to replace traits as the essential units for understanding personality differences. Today the influence of Personality and Situation on behaviours are seen by most researchers as having about equal weighting.[59]

Unlike personality traits, however, the Situation – Responses approach is changeable and as such is useful for the educator. Just as the marshmallow test has shown that executive function improves with practice, the Situational-Response behaviours too can be developed through training. – Mischel has provided us with a skill set that we use to develop our emotional responses and action. Rather than qualities of character he proposed the form of *personality signatures*. In his view, the individual's interpretation of the world is all important. Our action is fundamentally dependent on situational cues—the needs of a given situation- rather than being directly based on a set of categorised personality traits.[60] Behaviour is malleable, brains plastic. Just like willpower — far from being an innate trait- behaviour qualities can be taught, harnessed and enhanced.

Mischel developed the **Cognitive-Affective Model of personality** [61] that effectively explained the observed divergence in behaviours through the inter-connectedness of our encoding processes, behaviour generation processes and situations. Similar models were proposed by other prominent psychologists such Rotter, Dollard & Miller and Bandura in his social learning theory.[62] Another approach is a behavioural model first developed in the 1970s by psychologists Howard Gardner, Peter Salovey and John 'Jack' Mayer - that of Emotional Intelligence Theory (EI). Psychologists John D. Mayer and Peter Salovey first defined the phrase Emotional Intelligence" in the 1980s, which they defined as "the ability to monitor one's own and others' feelings and emotions, to discriminate among them and to use this information to guide ones thinking and actions."[63] EI rose to prominence in 1995 with the success of Daniel Goleman's book *"Emotional Intelligence: Why it Can Matter More Than IQ"*. The Mayer-Salovey Model is an abilities-based approach where EI is a skill that can be developed. The ability to perceive, understand, manage and use emotions to facilitate thinking and behaviour.

Daniel Goleman, later built on their work and produced a framework for emotional intelligence, which looks at how Awareness and Regulation of an individual can be developed to improve the sophistication of their behaviour in either internal or social contexts[64]. His argument was that higher levels of performance, wellbeing and hence personal success can result through smarter emotional behaviour.

Figure 5: Goleman's Initial Framework

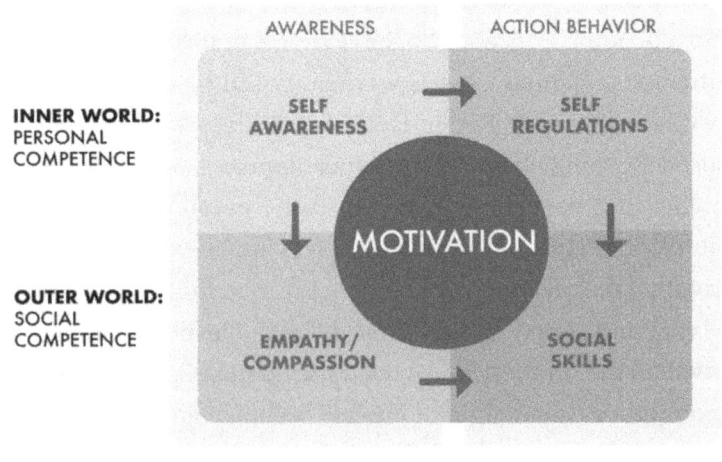

Figure 5 depicts Goleman's initial framework consisting of five elements. The first component of emotional intelligence theory is Awareness – how well do you know yourself and how aware are you of others? Executive function or Regulation is the second component, here referred to as Action through behaviour. How good is self-regulation and how does this impact on your thoughts, feelings and actions of others.

Central to the framework of emotional intelligence theory is the underlying drive - motivation. What form does this motivation take? Is effort expended on performance goals for self enhancement or in protecting internal consistency by avoiding challenge? Or is it used for learning goals for perceived success? The attitudes towards ability and the perceived value of education will certainly have a bearing on the direction of motivation levels. Goleman shows that personal potential can be realized by supporting the development of skills for emotional competence. How one controls the way they use their feelings and emotions are all skills that can be developed.

Adventure programs appear to be most effective at providing participants with a sense of self-regulation.[65] With the right people, places and processes Outdoor Adventurous learning aligns powerfully with Golemans' framework to successfully support the development emotional competence and hence some qualities of character.

AN ACTION SKILLSET

"You don't have time to teach Character? you don't have a choice – you are doing it all day long" Ron Berger

"There is nothing that holds us back from determining our own nature for ourselves, use the free will that we have been given
"Pico della Mirandola - On Human Dignity[1]

"Belonging to and actively participating in a school community is a deeply formative experience that helps students develop, amongst other things, their character. In a broad sense, character education permeates all subjects, wider school activities, and a general school ethos; it cultivates the virtues of character associated with common morality and develops students' understanding of what is excellent in diverse spheres of human endeavour. Schools should and do aid students in learning to know the good, love the good, and do the good..." (Jubilee Centre :2017)

All of us regardless of our political cultural and socioeconomic differences will value the qualities of respect, responsibility, courage and kindness. Whether by act or omission in our interpersonal relationships, goals and teaching practice we are representing such values each day. In this way an intentional and planned approach to character development is important to consider.

The semantic morass and ever evolving opinion on character and virtues makes it difficult to pin down character

---

[1] *Montaigne essayist and great renaissance influence largely unknow until the mid 20th Century.*

concepts without ending up with long lists of synonyms. In the end such learning comes through the adults and examples in our children's lives. It comes through their living life as it is.

In this chapter, I offer a focus skillset for developing awareness and purposeful action that arises from opportunities to experience action, reflect, communicate and understand better. Personal qualities then develop through practice in and out of school time. In other words, an individual's character is skillset of qualities that can be developed by living it and forms as part of an individual's interpretation of the world. Such skills become habitual and form qualities of character.

First however, it must be recognised that there is much need for a sound foundation in self-concept, self-regulation and self-efficacy. Children need first to understand about themselves and their purpose and meaning. As the child grows to understand about themselves, their character strengths, direction and aspiration emerge.

"Nobody has ever said to me they learned a positive character trait because of a curriculum or some 'sparkly pencil' that smells like strawberry's given being nice to the new kid" Prof. Marvin Berkowitz

As discussed earlier, Professor Mischel provided us with a set of behaviour conditioners[66] that we may use to develop our emotional responses and action. His Marshmallow test demonstrated that an individual's executive function improves with practice. Similarly, Mayer and Salovey showed us by developing abilities to perceive, understand and manage emotions we can improve thinking and behaviour.

In observing the differences in people's responses in a situation Mischel believed that the relative influence of situation variables and personal qualities can be determined. He detailed five personal variables that contribute to one's reaction to a situation detailed in Figure - 6. [67] Here, a personal skill has been associated with each of Mischel's behaviour modifiers. We could call then vital skills, soft skills, but as the intention for these to facilitate and support social action and behaviour qualities, I refer to them as "Action Skills". The four personal skills are the key components of Awareness and Regulation in Goleman's Framework in the last chapter. The Action Skills are all interrelated and evoke Authorship through focusing on Attention, Appreciation and Ability.

1. **Bringing to Attention:** Respect from self-control and mindfulness.
2. **Liberating Ability:** Courage from attitude and effort
3. **Generating Appreciation:** Resilience from gratitude.
4. **Providing Authorship:** Mastery from becoming independent and responsible

You know you have begun the journey when the student is beginning to listen deeply, to make connections and is becoming more aware. How often have you seen this occur in your practice? This is alone is feedback enough for any school leader. Relationships hinge upon this respect. With a foundation of greater awareness, we may bring the student to engage with life as it is now, as we would wish it to be. From this comes the generation of appreciation to drive their development. – a value for learning, a will to try and an intrinsic motivation to change.

The Action Skill Set depicted on the next page is proposed for young people to develop their juvenile levels of emotional skill and learning behaviours. It details our personal levels of attention, perceived ability and appreciation (Awareness) and personal levels of self-directed learning and authorship (Regulation). It is essentially a hybrid framework for developing qualities of character, based Goleman's and Michel's work. Here then is a pathway for positive action and character development for you to consider.[68]

Through appreciation and courage, a self-reinforcing cycle of prosocial behaviour and virtue emerges. In this way the action skills facilitate Emotional Intelligence and support practical wisdom, from this personal character development follows.

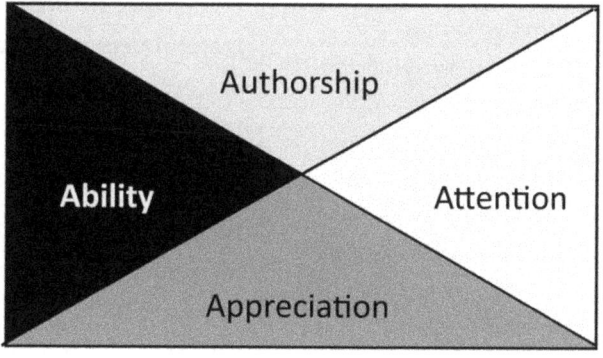

Figure 6: Framework for an Action Skill Set

Mischel's Behaviour Modifiers	Action Skill Set
1. Expectancies The expected results of different behaviours that are realized by the person inside their mind.	**Bringing to Attention:** To develop *Respect* from self-control and mindfulness.
2. Cognitive strategies The different perceptions of a specific event. For instance, what may be "threatening" for you may be "challenging" to another person	**Liberating Ability:** To enhance *Courage* from attitude and effort.
3. Competencies Our intellectual capabilities as well as social skills. 4. Subjective values The respective value of each possible outcomes of various behaviours.	**Generating Appreciation:** To increase *Resilience* from a grateful perspective and personal capability.
5. Self-regulatory systems The groups of rules and standards that people adapt to in order to regulate their behaviour	**Providing Authorship:** To support *Mastery* from becoming independent and responsible.

We all should support our children with deep experiences to develop their behaviour skills and social and emotional wellbeing. The Action Skill-Set when seen as a conscious target for mastery will not only improve our social emotional lives but will help us take a kindly view in our judgement of others too. Skills needed to become self-directed learners take time and require a context of purpose and engagement. We may best facilitate this through social action- here we may provide opportunities for authorship which, with greater awareness can help the school climate.

It is not inconceivable that through practice the child will find benevolent reinforcing spiral of behaviour. After all, it is through our cumulative decisions that we make the best of what we have been given in life. [69]

The remaining pages in Part Two then provide some short essays for each of the Action Skills as reflective examples. Part Three of this book then suggests ways the school environment and context can be enriched and how prosocial action has an important role to play in supporting the aspiration and fulfilment of children. Character education requires us to dig deeper and look at moral principles, ethos and virtues that underpin human behaviours.

As Dr Marvin Berkowitz (1997) claims: *"Effective character education is not adding a program or set of programs to a school. Rather it is a transformation of the culture and life of the school."*

A Skill Set for Action

BRING TO ATTENTION

- Awareness :- self, others & environment
- Focus :- present or future?
  - Problems or Solutions?
- Mind – still and controlled

LIBERATE ABILITY

- Mind-set for growth,
- Effort & Reward
- Failing forward.
- Avoiding procrastination

GENERATE APPRECIATION

- Prioritisation of values.
- Discerning the good
- Giving not taking
- Gratefulness & Abundance

PROVIDE AUTHORSHIP

- Self regulation,
- Mastery,
- Autonomy,
- Goals setting &
- Having purpose

SKILL 1: BRINGING TO ATTENTION

We take a handful of sand from the endless landscape of awareness around us and call that handful of sand the world." Robert Pirsig [70]

Nothing matters so much as when you think about it. What we bring to our attention impacts our experiences. The experiencing self is how you feel right now. The role of our attention is central to what we experience. Consider someone in love who is stuck in a traffic jam, how they experience this as opposed to someone who is depressed. The role of attention is central to endogenous happiness – the wellbeing that comes from our living and immediate thinking about it. A large study of US and French women on how they spent their day showed that they both spent approximately the same amount of time eating. However, they were significantly different in wellbeing measures, with the French being happier. The difference was that the French women spent more of that time focusing on enjoying their eating than their American counterparts.

We live an anticipation, we are always rushing to move onto the next thing. Part of our species extraordinary capacity is its ability to commit complicated tasks to unconscious pre-programmed skills, e.g. when driving a car. (We can master this most complicated tasks moving from a conscious deliberate exercise to an unconscious automatic skill). Our attention then, is hampered by our mind's rush to commit experiences to existing gestalt groupings and to commit new tasks to unconsciousness. For our *experiencing self* however, this means that giving one's attention to a moment is not as easy as it seems. It is a skill to master. To be aware is to see. We must wake up to the immediate moment.

Nobel Laureate, Daniel Kahneman says we cannot think of any circumstance that affects our happiness without it distorting its importance. For example, consider a person sharing a story of a music concert they went to which had great music but how the whole performance was ruined because at the end there was a terrible screeching sound. Despite the thirty minutes of wonderful music, they were left with a memory of how it was ruined. What was ruined was not the experience, but the memories of the experience. What we remember is a weighted average of the peak experience and end experience. Everything else pails into significance. His thesis is that we each have two-selves. Our *remembering self* is not the same as our *experiencing self*. The memory of an experience is what we keep from our living. It is unique to us and it changes over time as it is recalled. It is our remembering self that guides our choices.

If we are consumed with ourselves we will never see the marvellous every day details- such as the shimmer of ripples, a refracted spectrum of colour, or a tree casting dancing shadows. Underwhelmed by ourselves we live underwhelmed by the little wonders of the world. Awe helps us experience a bigger view – a bigger frame - in how can see ourselves. Through wonderment we too feel our own inherent value of just being.

Watching sunrise through our mobile phone camera rather than just experiencing it. We have become digital witnesses.

Our attempts to capture everything and to chronologise onto online timelines takes us away from being fully mindful in the moment and withdraws some of the appreciation of 'just being' with the temporal moment.

It's true our memory is fallible, but how can the fumbling efforts to capture a phone photograph compare to the full engagement with a personally significant moment captured by an immediacy that can never be repeated.

Avoiding Procrastination

"The future is always ideal: The fridge is stocked, the weather clear, the train runs on schedule and meetings end on time. Today, well, stuff happens."- Hara Estroff Marano [71]

In the pursuit of newsworthy stories our popular media generally seek out people of interest. This norm has led to generations of our students only seeing the people who are at "their summit" being proclaimed and roundly praised. What is not shown are the thousands of hours of their hard work, sacrifice, uncertainty, luck and dedication taken to get to that point. This is perhaps one of the most insidious influences on the young mind. This media bias has supported a culture of celebrity worship, short termism and procrastination.

Procrastination manifests itself within every aspect of modern life. We all know life would improve if we would buckle down and put in the effort – the question is a matter of when? The future value of one action is seen as less valuable than the short-term (more immediate) reward of another action. In practice, this means the easier (and often more hedonistic) option of short-term reward will outweigh long-term goals.

This "Live for Now" mentality stands in opposition to the goals and essential functions for health and wellbeing - a cause for unhealthy behaviours and lost opportunities. The trick is to accept the *present self* will not be the person facing those choices, it will be the *future self.* To share with our children, we can say *"The choices I make today shape the life of my future self"*. There is a sense of accountability for making more from the moment. What we do now makes for tomorrow. The procrastinator will keep staring at the blank canvas and though they may entertain the glamour of potential they are simply held back from achieving anything. We all face the hurdle of procrastination, allowing self-consciousness and doubt to hold back our potential, when all that is required is the discipline to begin and to keep on going.

Mindfulness and the Art of Outdoor Education.

The word Mindfulness originally comes from the Sanskrit word smriti, which means remember. Zen Teacher Thich Nhat Hanh advises "Mindfulness is remembering to come back to the present moment". This is an ongoing process that is not limited to a particular time, moment or action. The understanding of Mindfulness has become so diluted in recent years that today the word has lost much of this original meaning.

76

Most of us – outdoor practitioners included – spend so much time bouncing between the thoughts of the past and the future that we lose touch with what's happening right here, right now. This prevents us from appreciating the deep mystery of being alive. Encouraging self-reflection, adding thinking time to our course planning and even 'letting the mountains speak for themselves' are all tried and tested methods oft used by outdoor practitioners to create time for our students to truly immerse themselves; physically, mentally and spiritually within the environment which we have chosen for that very purpose. It is therefore no surprise that personal and social development is an aim and outcome for almost every outdoor practitioner across the industry.

So you're telling me I should be more 'mindful'. Why? Basically mindfulness is one method with which we can regain our attentional focus in our lives, whether this is at work or beyond. An understanding of 'Mindfulness' can help our children filter out all the concerns and preconceptions they have about their past and their future; this in turn could allow them to immerse themselves and engage to a much deeper level in the experiences we can facilitate.

The principles of 'mindfulness' and compassion are central to Zen practice and philosophy and this aligns nicely with the more enlightened views of experiential education (outdoor therapy in particular) so warrants further investigation. Mindfulness, as a way of life or a methodology to work with, could easily be interpreted as being fully present not just on the river or climb but throughout the rest of the day as well. The key is not just to sit and calm your mind but to learn to read and react effectively in any situation based on what's happening at that very moment.

"The habit of ignoring our present moments in favour of others yet to come leads directly to a pervasive lack or awareness of the web of life in which we are embedded" Kabat-Zinn 'Wherever You Go, There You Are'.

Courtesy of Andy Thorpe, Learning Adventure Manager, The Outward Bound Trust.

SKILL 2: LIBERATING ABILITY

"I am only one, but I am one. I cannot do everything, but I can do
something. And I will not let what I cannot do interfere with what I can do"
– Edward Everett Hale.

"Because you are alive, everything is possible"
- Thich Nhat Hanh[72]

There is a clear relationship between a person's expectations and their levels of esteem, with how they choose to participate. In liberating our student's ability, we should lift them from those thoughts and approaches that lower expectations for them. This is something that children learn from their earliest primary experiences and family context. Beliefs about a fixed level of ability can provide a convenient excuse to avoid challenge and supports the development of defensive self-enhancement strategies in children.

One of the first to look at attitudes towards self-value and behaviour was the American psychologist William James. He first coined the term 'self-esteem' in his Principles of Psychology (1890).

James defined our self-worth as being determined by the amount of success we have, divided by how high our expectations are. We can feel better about ourselves by succeeding in the world but also by adjusting the level of our expectations and hopes.[73]

In other words, according to James,

"Success" = Self-Esteem x Expectations

Figure 4 depicts this relationship as a Model of Expectation and Self Esteem. The emphasis on esteem and success remains widely held and popular today. Many parents and teachers value positive reinforcement and act to avoid negative consequence in the hope of increased happiness and achievement for their children. Today one will find most Outdoor Activity Providers offering "increased levels of self-esteem" as one of their key outcomes.

Figure 8: James's Model of Expectations & Self Esteem

	Complacency	Success
	Failure	Demoralisation
	Low - Expectations - High	

(Self-Esteem - High to Low on vertical axis)

This became popularised in the 1960s when research supported a movement for increasing self-esteem. Part of this development were programmes that actively attempted to increase self-esteem in the classroom to raise student performance and behaviours.[74]

"Since the 1969 publication of The Psychology of Self-Esteem, in which Nathaniel Branden opined that self-esteem was the single most

important facet of a person... Anything potentially damaging to kids' self-esteem was axed. Competitions were frowned upon. Soccer coaches stopped counting goals and handed out trophies to everyone. Teachers threw out their red pencils. Criticism was replaced with ubiquitous, even undeserved praise." (Branson: 2007) [75]

In the last two decades psychologists have distanced themselves from the "self-esteem movement". Some of its practices have now been seen to have had adverse effects on children's emotional development. Research in the late 1990s suggested that praise can hold paradoxical effects on a child's perception of their own ability in the classroom.[76] The artificial boosting of self-esteem may lower subsequent performance.[77] When praise is deemed to be false by a child or is trait based it holds negative effects. More recently, we know praising children may come at the price of resilience.[78] The relationship between efficacy, expectations and outcomes is thus not as straight forward as William James' model would have us expect. The relationship between our beliefs about intelligence and our approach to participation and learning is more self reinforcing and complicated. Figure 8 shows how the reinforcing cyclic nature of esteem works in conjunction with expectations and self-perception. Our feelings and thoughts about challenge and our ability, frame how we react to situations. The decision on how we engage and what we get out of the situation feeds back as a confirmation of self-image. The energy that goes into Self Enhancement strategies and diversion is part of the effort to protect self-esteem. What can work as either a self-reinforcing upwards cycle of positive feedback, can equally work as means to a negative downward cycle to disengagement and low levels of aspiration. Different confidence levels impact behaviour outcomes. This model was based on the work of Professor Carol Dweck. As a distinguished researcher she has become internationally well known for her work on motivation and learning success. Her work brought light and insight into the paradoxes of praise. Over the last thirty years her research has shown how personal attitudes have the power to restrict or transform levels of engagement. She has shown how the beliefs we hold about ourselves profoundly affect the way we lead our lives. One example of an attitude that prevents us from engaging with challenge arises from the beliefs we hold about intelligence. When children feel their worth is contingent on their behaviour or academic performance, they see challenge as personally threatening, fear failure, and grow anxious to please. This belief makes them less resilient learners. A child might believe they will never be able to achieve in learning, often due to a quasi-genetic excuse passed onto them that they are unable to improve their intelligence through effort. It may be an off-hand comment from someone respected or those in authority who may voice or imply regressive views - believing ability as immutable and predictive. Importantly, we all hold this type of fixed thinking at different times and in different respects, but none are more susceptible to it than the children who look to us. It does not have to be this way. Dweck's research shows us that mindsets can change the terms of engagement for students and that the change in mindset was readily learnable. Many students who had seen school as a place where they performed and were judged, now had a way to understood that they too had an active role to play in the development of their own minds.

Figure 9: Beliefs, Expectation and Achievement Behaviour

Grateful for Sean Comiskey for this Frame. Influenced by Dweck, C. S. (1986).[79]

A Mindset for Success

"Most educational reforms focus on curriculum and pedagogy what material is taught and how it is taught. However, curriculum and pedagogy have often been narrowly defined as the academic content and students' intellectual processing of that material. Research shows that this is insufficient. In our pursuit of educational reform, something essential has been missing: the psychology of the student. Psychological factors — often called motivational or non-cognitive factors — can matter even more than cognitive factors for students' academic performance. These may include students' beliefs about themselves, their feelings about school, or their habits of self-control." (Dweck, Walton, Cohen: 2014). [80]

A high stakes testing culture that only values final drafts will never accommodate the necessary motivation, behaviours or respect for supporting a student's greatest potential. In liberating ability, we must see that the learning becomes the end in itself. In life, there is no final draft.

A growth mindset is a mindset for success, it is more than just a means to self-efficacy. It asks us to focus on progress, to give space to develop strategies, and to give our best efforts. Students will adopt learning goals, will take necessary risks and won't overly worry about failure because each mistake becomes a chance to learn. We should see that agency for learning is in our student's hands and their attitudes are supported with a love of the journey.

Qualities of character arise when we are in the midst of the learning journey. It is when we are busy with the process that we have the capacity to liberate ability through agency and attitude. It is not just for the sake of the performance or intellectual virtues either. This opportunity is as much for the development of moral virtues such as empathy, humility, altruism - which emerge when facing difficulty with courage and good heart.

"The hallmark of the mastery-oriented pattern is a tendency to focus on the process (effort or strategy) when faced with difficulty. In addition, children displaying the mastery oriented response maintain their expectations, positive affect, and positive self-assessments and continue to exhibit constructive behaviour when a setback occurs." (Kamins & Dweck: 1999). [81]

The significance of mindsets for learning and attraction of the apparent simplicity of the concept[82] has inadvertently created a new popular movement with educators hungry for quick results. Since 2010 the term "growth mindset" has grown rapidly in use. Now a familiar term in classrooms that some schools even set about testing children for it! Recent practice in education has sought out short cut interventions without regard for the complexity or the requisite psychology involved.

"A lot of educators think I'll give a lesson on growth mindset and that will be it, rather than embodying it in their teaching and infiltrating it through the whole culture of the classroom," C.S. Dweck. [83]

The false use of mindsets overlooks the principal implication of Dweck's work - it asks for a reappraisal of goals in educational achievement. Those schools invested in the transmission approach -who only seek to weigh attainment - should not be surprised that their attempted interventions are unsuccessful. Their league tabling is just another way of messaging the same sense of contingent worth as seen in early childhood.[84] If the process is only regarded as a means to an end, then the message is lost.   A deeper appreciation asks more of the school- a cultural solution rather than a quick fix or an off-the shelf solution. We must respect how motivational processes influence a child's acquisition, transfer, and use of knowledge. An impact not only on attainment but on more effective socialisation.

"Mindset change is not about picking up a few pointers here and there. It's about seeing things in a new way. When people change to a growth mindset, they change from a judge-and-be-judged framework to a learn-and-help-learn framework. Their commitment is to growth, and growth takes plenty of time, effort, and mutual support." (Dweck: 2007) [85]

The Perception of Ability

As Eva stepped closer to the edge of Aberdovey jetty a group of school children watched on in trepidation. She was about to take a step off a 17-foot peer into the swirling sea below. There was a current and the instructional staff were all tentative, ready to support her in the last challenge of the week.

The okay is given, and Eva confidently strode out into space - off and down into the water. The onlookers, who themselves, are about to do the jump were full of admiration and amazement, more so than you would ever think. Eva was partially blind.

Student after student from Team Tenzing - took on the challenge of jetty jump. It was the last day of their week-long course. All eight from New College Worcester- a residential college for the visually impaired, jumped from the jetty's heights. As the students from Team Tenzing put away their kit, the nervous onlookers from the next group to take on the jetty jump, are overheard saying, "well if the blind kids can do it then there's no excuse for me".

It is easy to think, "oh these students will have to do easier challenges in comparison to 'normal groups' as they can't see". But time after time during the week, with a progression to the level of challenge, their achievements were great. It is all too easy to think those with a disability should do adventures which are different to what you may do with fully able-bodied students. We all know everyone has a different perception of risk, but to what extend to we project our fears on onto others? As educators and parents, we should be mindful as to our perception of ability and mindful as to the individual differences in the perception of challenge.

We are all expert in making assumptions as to what someone is like... but then aren't we blinded according to our own preconceptions? The hard reality for the students today is that societies attitude towards their ability is their greatest disability – not sight. The likelihood is that Eva and her students will not gain opportunities for employment in their life due to the limiting assumptions of others. In many ways such societal limitations are the greatest challenge to the students of Team Tenzing.

We strive to challenge all students physically and mentally during their course. Tutors gain experience throughout their career in delivering experiences which will challenge each individual within the group. When instructing a course of visually impaired students, this perception of what the students' abilities will be needs to be reflected in the plan for the week - or does it? The levels of vision amongst the students varied from blurred vision in one eye, to total blindness. When faced with scrambling, climbing, abseiling, jumping from a power boat or from the jetty, these differences in visual ability made no difference to the undertaking the challenges, or learning. This makes me wonder, why onlookers were in awe at Team Tenzing. Eva and her classmate's actions represented a direct challenge to the onlookers – Eva's actions addressed the onlooker's own preconceptions of personal ability. Her action spoke clearly - "Don't measure me by your own perceived limitations, I am too am able!" Just as Eva was a source of awe in action, don't you think we should also be that bit more courageous in seeing others' potential too?

Courtesy of Jo Fromant, Senior Instructor, & with thanks to Phil Bresnan and Caroline Gibbs from New College Worcestershire

"Your disability is your opportunity"

Kurt Hahn believed we should 'teach' children how to overcome their weaknesses. The concept of triumphing over adversity is an important theme in his philosophy:

"Make children meet with triumph and defeat. After you have replenished their tanks of vitality, by discovering and maintaining their strengths, but not before, you should tackle their weaknesses. It is possible to wait on a child's inclinations and gifts and arrange carefully for an unbroken series of successes. You may make him or her happy that way – I doubt it – but you certainly cripple him for the battle of life. It is our business to plunge the children into enterprises in which they are likely to fail, and we may not hush up that failure; but we should teach them to overcome defeat. "To him that over cometh will I give to eat of the tree of life"... Success in the sphere of one's weakness is often as great a source of satisfaction as triumph in the sphere of one's talents" - *Kurt Hahn, 1934[86]*

SKILL 3: GENERATING APPRECIATION

"When we are constantly wishing for something we overlook everything we already have" - Alfred Adler

"Dead people receive more flowers than the living ones because the regret is stronger than gratitude" – Anna Frank

Typically, we do not appreciate any moment in isolation. Whether it is the frame of the experience, our physiological state, emotional state, or reference to the past, we weave the threads of context into the fabric of present judgement.

The memory of an experience is what we keep from our living experience. It is unique to us and it changes each time it is recalled, gradually modified by our context. It is our remembering self that guides our choices.

One's memory is affected by their knowledge of the world. We fit our recollections into general outlines or Schemas, filling in various gaps in memory without knowing that we do so. Each little distortion in recall becomes part of the fabric of the memory.

Numerous experiments[87] document the claim that memories for events are strongly affected by the framework of prior knowledge *in terms of which they are understood.* For example:

In one study, participants were asked to take one of two different viewpoints: that of a prospective homebuyer or that of a

burglar. They were then asked to read a description of a family home.

The different perspectives affected what was later recalled. In the case of the 'home buyers' it was, a leaky roof. In the case of the 'burglars' it was a valuable coin collection.[88]

This example demonstrates that by asking participants to take on a certain view point, such as relating to a particular perspective in their life, we may prime a powerful frame prior to the experience. With this we can evoke a receptiveness that may not already be there- we may frame for gratefulness, for what we have, for what we can change and for what we must accept.

Sensible Self-denial Increases Wellbeing

Challenge demands us to stretch out and leave the inertia of our comfort zone. It will require effort, the chance of failure and may involve a perceived risk to our reputation. Exercising a choice in which comfort may be sacrificed draws upon parallels in other areas. Where expressing a discipline over inertia or for some courage over fears lead to positive esteem and worth. Consider the metaphor that can be drawn with going on a winter mountain expedition, or from taking on more responsibilities. In sacrificing time as service to others, or in sharing, giving up comforts, in the discipline of duty, in practising a skill, in overcoming mortifications as cold and rain, we improve ourselves.

"Hardship and discomfort, which are unavoidable once committed to the river, are potentially at odds with holiday expectations of relaxation, discretionary time, and comfort. The

unavoidable physicality of the trip was a recurring theme in participant comments... Almost without exception these potential disappointments were not a source of dissatisfaction. On the contrary, framing the trip as a wilderness expedition transformed the hardships into signifiers of authenticity, and thus testaments to the virtuousness of the wilderness experience". Kagan (1998, p. 153). Kagan argues: "the affirmation of virtue takes precedence over the search for sensory pleasure most of every day" Virtuous privation trumps pleasure, and satisfaction is not simply an index of enjoyment. The moral values attributed to the experience [are] diverse".[89]

As people grow accustomed to more comforts and more material goods (e.g. fine dining, new smartphones), they often experience "hedonic adaptation" — that is, they get used to the finer things and are less inclined to savour daily pleasures. How can people avoid the trap of hedonic adaptation? Interestingly, scarcity can lead people to focus on enjoying an experience more deeply (i.e. savouring), which increases happiness. In one sense, it may not be surprising that self-denial makes people long for the thing they cannot have. Yet research by Quoidbach and Dunn shows that these people are actually happier in the end in part because they savour more. In a world where often, greater availability does not lead to positive feelings and improved wellbeing absence may make us fonder for the things we cannot have in the moment, leading to greater happiness and a greater appreciation of them in the end.[90]

THE IMPACT OF GRATITUDE

*Framing outdoor experiences for transformational learning
& wellbeing.*

"This is a story about an expedition with a youth group to a remote Hebridean Island off the Scottish coast. The group leader, Tim, was a patient fellow – he needed to be. The group struggled to get on. The first days were full of moaning and complaining, petty arguments and selfishness. It was not a happy group of youths. They didn't like working together; they didn't want to be there. They were hard work. After the third day they had eaten all their food. They came to Tim and the other leaders saying, "we have run out of food, what are you going to do?"

Well, since the team were on the far side of the island and their return transport was a fishing boat that would not return for another 4 days. Tim's answer was pretty simple... "nothing". The Students realised that there was nothing that could be done! The boat couldn't come early to change this situation. The reality hit home to the students - they will have to come up with a solution!

The group had a serious problem, one that they created and that couldn't be escaped from. They began to panic. Eventually once the emotion and anger had subsided; when they accepted things, they started to talk. They talked to each other in a way they had never done before – the calamity had broken down all facades – they spoke to each other like warm hearted humans. When they thought together, one or two students came out with food they had brought with them but were hiding away secret for personal pleasure. Then, one went through the bin and found even more - nearly full packets

93

of food they previously had thrown away. To their surprise there was more than enough food...they became more joyful each time they found things, the students started to buzz, they began to help each other and get along.

Something changed in the students – there were no more arguments, there was a sense of purpose, they became kinder and happier as they began to rejoice in the smallest of triumphs.

Bound with purpose, they had no option to quit...and so began a change in perspective that led them to sufficiency, happiness and lasting friendships. They became grateful for the small everyday things and found this a source of abundance."

I initially called his story Famine to Feast as it highlighted to me how much we can change our circumstances. Over the duration of my own instructing I thought about this experience when working with my own students.

It seemed to me at times, that some of our children behave as if they too were short of resources. Not a famine of food but of belief. A world view with little confidence in effort, little hope in ability, little will to persevere, no belief in change. Some students clearly seemed to be in survival mode of sorts, for an acceptance, recognition and to get credit. There is no time for selflessness, for humility or empathy. Wouldn't that be for those who have given up? - or (paradoxically), those who are already abundantly well to do, "famous" even? By losing their easy escape back to "normality", the students in the story were impelled to recognise the many things they had previously taken for granted. They had to find resources within themselves. Reality became immediate. The value of those everyday things became apparent only once they had been taken away.

Gratitude is a way of thinking that can turn disaster into a stepping stone. By realising that the power one has to transform an obstacle into an opportunity is personally liberating. Gratitude reframes a potential loss into something of assured hope. Without hope change is spiritually inconceivable.[91] Gratitude recasts negativity into positive channels for pragmatic action which, by its very definition, is practical and solution focused.

A significant behaviour change happened in the students over the following days– the students invested time on each other – they took opportunity to be of service to each other. They became more giving. The spirit of the group moved into a new frame of gratefulness.

Time and memory remould reality nearer to the heart's desire.[92] So is it not important to start here first? – By scrutinising the frame which we adopt – those assumptions which have a powerful hold on our ultimate behaviours to self, others and the environment. Should we not first fix the vices before building upon virtues? By looking at gratitude we address the spirit. According to Robert Emmons[93] there are five possible obstacles to living a grateful life:

1. Pervasive negativity– Our natural attentiveness to bad news
2. A sense of entitlement – a cult of celebrity and obsession with self.
3. Making comparisons- focusing on what we don't have
4. Apathy, boredom and fear- Laziness & Insecurities.

5.   Lack of effort – seeing effort as being a sign of weakness.

As practitioners we certainly recognise these in the groups we work with. They haven't changed for more than the seventy years since Kurt Hahn wrote of the declines of modern youth. For Hahn a life of service was to be the beneficial outcome. Indeed, service is the ultimate outcome of a life of gratitude

Typically, we do not address our own thinking until challenged to do so. We take a lot of things as givens and we do not question norms. We need *to pierce through* our relationship to the assumptions that surround us By facilitating opportunities for our students to do exactly this we provide for high impact transformational learning.

The students in the story were faced by a real challenge and this was the source of great dissonance. They had to address their own thinking and ways of behaving. The disjuncture was an assault on their assumed values. Through reflection the students individually processed their own situation, it led to reconsidered behaviour (some admitted the error of their ways and others began to share their precious chocolate). Importantly however the deepest impact, they addressed their own assumed values – they unlocked a personally lasting change in doing so. In finding their own solution over the following days, they tested their new-found values and saw how helpful and liberating this way of being was. Gratitude worked on a personal level, so they kept on doing it.

As the students discovered, gratitude offered an opportunity to reappraise their situation more positively. For

Dewey experiential learning is a consequence of both 'trying' and 'undergoing.' Therefore, the meaning of an experience cannot be accounted for sufficiently with a simplistic emphasis upon reflection after the experience.[94] Dewey's theory implores us to engage with the whole experience as we live it. Dewey emphasized the experiential learning cycle as follows:

'...first, that the pupil have a genuine situation of experience - that there be a continuous activity in which he is interested for its own sake; secondly, that a genuine problem develop within this situation as a stimulus to thought; third, that he possess the information and make the observations needed to deal with it; fourth, that suggested solutions occur to him which he shall be responsible for developing in an orderly way; fifth, that he have the opportunity and occasion to test his ideas by application, to make their meaning clear and to discover for himself their validity.'

(Dewey: 1916), This is depicted in Figure 10. As suggested by Dewey, in order to become our *'Best Self'* we must continually reappraise and adjust. Our life is a cycle of becoming. Over and over again, we have the possibility to reinvent ourselves.

Expressing gratitude enhances the shared experience and the greater the number of people expressing sincere feeling of appreciation the more persistent people will feel positive.[95] Fortunately framing for gratitude can be quite straight forward - two methods for getting students to express gratitude are:

1. *Think about someone to whom they were grateful for* – Get students to answer generally at the start of the day and then move the attention to the team after their adventurous activity.

2. *Use descriptors – get students to describe something in their surroundings that they are grateful for*. At the start of the day ask the students "what do they love?" You will be surprised to see how they move from loving their mobile phone in the morning to describing their love of the blue sky or sunlight on the water after a great adventure on a sunny day... it will be their waterproofs on other days!

Figure 10: The Dewey Cycle of Becoming

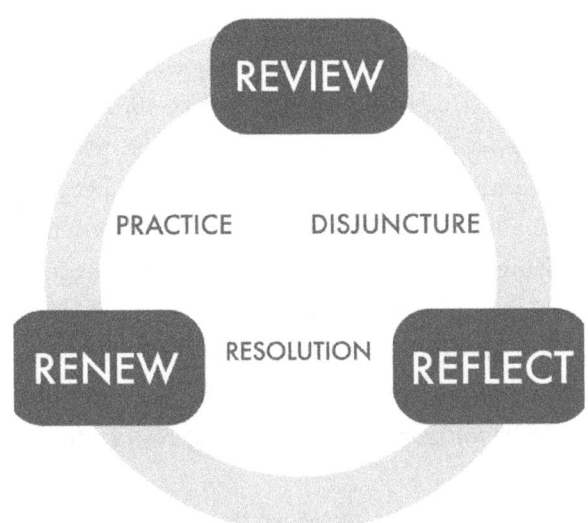

Living with a frame of gratefulness is liberating. To begin to look at the things we have, what our strengths are and what is working in our lives, provides for a mindset of abundance. The benefits of an abundant mindset includes' greater satisfaction from relationships, higher levels of trust and inclusion, higher levels of effort and authentic behaviour that is aligned with personal values. With *a mindset of abundance*, people are less likely to fear failure and are more resilient in the face of uncertainty.[96]

You don't have to find yourself stranded on an island in order to find such transformational moments. You can build gratitude into your practice, starting with your own personal example. e.g. see how well it works out when you do so. Keep it simple. If it works do more if it! In doing, it is not so much a matter of solving problems but dissolving problems. Let's focus on the positive and what's possible where we are right now.

Life continually asks of us what we are to be. In turn we continually recreate ourselves through our choice of action. Through the freedoms of gratefulness, we become abundant in our approach to life. We become the authors of our lives; not of a good life, but of a *beautiful* life - now isn't that a journey we should all take!

SKILL 4: PROVIDING AUTHORSHIP

"Meanings lie inside of people and cannot be directly manipulated and controlled. Learning only occurs when something happens inside the learner and this is, for the most part, in his, not the teacher's, control."
Abraham Maslow, Perceiving & Behaving P69

Author: -as a verb the word originates from "to do" .
As a noun the word stems from Latin & old French Auctor, - creator, originator, instigator, progenitor, builder, founder, authority, performer, doer, responsible person, literally "one who causes to grow" [97]

The traditional idea of school is that the learner learns from the teacher, and that the imparted knowledge then leads to such opportunity and through wealth, their emancipation. However employability and the creation of opportunity depends not just on knowledge, skills and attitudes, but how one is able to use their personal assets, and how they present them to employers. Are we equipping students with emotional skills to help them succeed in their lives? In jobs that perhaps don't even exist yet? There is need to understand and engage with different forms and networks of power and knowledge. In the education of our children should we not grow skills to allow for better decision making, empathy and social responsibility? Underpinning high impact learning is personal authorship.

The traditional or *transmission view* of learning together with the drive towards evidence-based teaching, leads to a form of *educational positivism* – i.e. a belief we can control and predict human performance. The decision on learning strategy is then implicitly sought out in the organisation's best interest not necessarily the child's.[98] The focus is on exam results rather than values. If it gets results it is good. Policy makers have historically left educators risk averse unable to provide for society or employer needs.

To allow students to hold the power in deciding the degree to which they want their own learning to be "weak" or "strong" jeopardises the school's outcomes. Even though it is widely known that increasing the degree of student involvement in decision making in learning enhances motivation, autonomy is quashed. *There is subject content to get through and exams to sit.* Providing the learner with more autonomy places the organisation at risk.

"The idea of 'becoming educationally wise', …is about the whole person (educationally speaking), not merely an acquisition of knowledge, skills and dispositions; it involves the development of a person who makes wise judgements. This can only be developed through the use of practical judgement and preferably through engagement with others in a number of different ways" Gert Biesta[99]

We can better support a move towards self-directed learning, maturity and engagement with positive relationships Those essential skills which Kurt Hahn highlighted affect personal and emotional wellbeing as well as attitudes to resilience, responsibility and respect. Regardless of the task we all need to feel that we have the capacity to accomplish the task or the courage to try. When the work is purposeful and relevant motivation flows. The prevailing attitudes and beliefs of students need to be developed to allow the possibility of Authorship. It takes time and some stability in teacher/ student relationships - two resources which, in times of austerity, many schools struggle to find.

... 'wisdom is particularly important in order to [ensure] that our educational actions are never just a repetition of what has happened in the past but are always radically open toward the future. We need judgment rather than recipes in order to be able to engage with this openness and do so in an educational way.' (p.137) Gert Biesta (2014) Learning Space — Review of 'The Beautiful Risk of Education'

Self-Directed Learning asks for the individual to take the initiative and the responsibility for their learning. Although this degree of autonomy demands maturity, there is no reason why all children cannot experience and develop the skills at a level matching their ability. Figure 11 suggests four stages in learner engagement, progressively developing towards the skilled, self-motivated, proactive learner. As the level of skills develop it becomes more feasible to allow a transfer of responsibility and autonomy from the teacher to the learner. A learner continuum is formed, with the two approaches towards learning sitting at each end. There is a balance to be struck in the classroom which is political – on one side, the traditional teacher directed model and on the other end balances the Self-directed model. Rather than being a static framework this shows the possible landscape from which we can grow a sense of Authorship in our students.

In the same way that physical activity in a natural environment and experiencing awe are invaluable, so too are the smaller daily opportunities in the classroom context.

Strategies of accountability, peer feedback and support for academic maturity (such as the Crew circle provides) are important moving through this continuum towards a more self-directed and autonomous learning environment. Relationship is key.

There are many commercial learning power programmes available in the education market. Regardless of their ingenuity, if they are not accompanied with opportunities to delegate levels of student responsibility and negotiate accountability they quickly wither and become just another form of control. What is being lost through the emphasis on empiricism- and which needs to be rediscovered - is the *professional judgement* of teachers and space to develop positive dialogue and trust in their relationships with students.

Figure 11: A Learner Continuum Towards Mastery

	TEACHER		STUDENT	

Stage>	1 Dependent	2 Involved	3 Committed	4 Self-Directed
Respect	I am punctual and bring the right equipment	I take responsibility for my performance	I put in my best effort, take pride in my work.	I listen to others and respect their opinion, I seek to understand.
Courage	I contribute thoughtful ideas in lessons	I ask relevant questions to develop my understanding	I am not afraid to take risks and make mistakes	I endeavour to succeed & grow despite failures
Resilience	I can manage distractions, can focus my attention.	I make the most of available resources and know how to get assistance.	I can plan my time to meet deadlines and reduce stress	I persevere in the face of difficult task
Mastery	I seek examples of excellent work and look to emulate	I can critique my work for Strengths & Weaknesses	I give time and effort for quality, for critique & redraft.	I can set goals and work by them to meet success criteria

Here we see the relationship between the possible level of student ownership and the level of requited teacher support. This is essentially a reframing of the Tannenbaum and Schmidt Leadership Continuum 100 which depicts the relationship between the level of freedom that a manager chooses to give to a team and the level of authority they choose to use. Whereas Tannenbaum& Schmidt seek to model appropriate management style, the aim here is to delegate accountability in learning.

VIRTUES FOR LIFE

Although the term "Outward Bound" is now generically used by many when referring to outdoor activities it is unfortunately the case that the activities often have little in common with what a course from The Outward Bound Trust or International licensed schools actually entails. The more knowledgeable educator might describe an Outward Bound course as a wilderness-based leadership course. However, Kurt Hahn's educational vision was to train students through the wilderness, not for it. As our Chairman, HRH Duke of York, said at The OB Education forum at Buckingham Palace in October 2017 *"It's not about Tents!"* It's vital that this distinction is made as it underscores the educational vision and mission for the Trust. The Outward Bound Trust exists to challenge students in a way that promotes the following virtues:

Compassion
- *To show understanding, care, love and pride for ourselves and for other people*
- *To be committed to contributing positively to our community*
- *To help others achieve*

Courage
- *To put ourselves outside our comfort zone to develop and deepen or learning and character*
- *To have conviction in our thoughts and feelings and communicate them effectively*
- *To endeavor to succeed, even though there is a chance of failure*

Mastery
- *To strive be one's best self, in discipline & determination*
- *Give time and effort for quality, for critique & redraft. To strive to create beautiful work as a craftsman would.*

Respect
- *To respect ourselves and others*
- *To work with others despite differences or difficulties*
- *To show consideration towards other people and our environment*

Resilience
- *To be self-motivated to achieve our best*
- *To be resilience, responsibility and a never give up attitude*
- *To recognise the reasons for failure and, as a result, enhance our chances for success*

Figure 12: Hahn's Pillars of Character

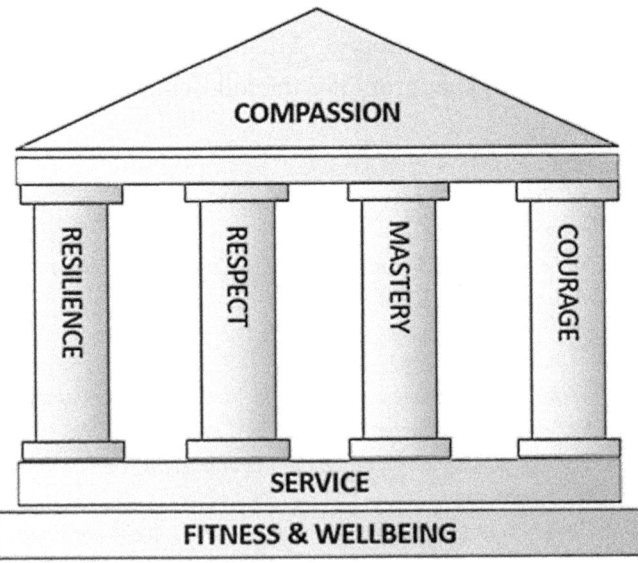

PART THREE

HIGH IMPACT LEARNING

MAKING CONNECTIONS

"Every adventurer starts out as ...a storyteller who wants to believe his own stories, and therefore needs to act them out. In this sense, the escape from culture becomes a coy act of culture..." - Zweig, P. (1981) The Adventurer, p. 240.

"Education must enable young people to effect what they have recognized to be right, despite hardships, despite dangers, despite inner skepticism, despite boredom and despite mockery from the world" – Kurt Hahn

As unique as people, in culture, no one school is the same. Every school has its own narrative, whether explicit or not. To some, it is their brand, a most precious bit of capital, whilst sadly to others, it's a millstone. Each student, cohort and year group writes that narrative – implicitly the messages from the school are incorporated into their contract. We should not impose the school's vision upon the individual without capturing their hearts.

Learning through relationships is a root of the curriculum, it is through relationships that culture, skill and knowledge is transferred. Any change in the organisational priorities of a school will impact the learning culture.[100] Engaging both teacher and students equally in the co-writing of their small society allows values to collaboratively emerge. Derived from curriculum, the notion of the verb *Currere* allows for this space in the relationship,[101] (literal definition stems from Latin, in which it means "to run"). To run with students' interests, to refocus attention away from the impersonal goals of mandated curriculum is at times essential for emerging virtues in children. Allowing the teacher and student to move through the milieu is key to authentic and caring relationship. The role of the teacher as mediator for the school is thus a most important means for sharing values. Yet so few schools invest time to induct and inspire their staff into ways of being which bring the school's mission alive.

Let's give students the opportunity to act for a concern bigger than themselves. Too many children haven't had the essential experiences in life to make sense of opportunities. Consider the apathy of learned helplessness of many students. The tendency to think "not me, someone else..." Before we lock into the individual and attend to their need, consider the culture that informs them. Is this behaviour merely an osmosis of powerlessness cued from a passive TV watching, exam sitting world? In society as in schools, culture is continuously informing us. The social norms of urban modernity pervade every aspect of a young person's life. They adopt these norms unknowingly from all around them. Some are positive, such as pluralism and egalitarianism, however many less so. Michael Foley in his book, *The Age of Absurdity: Why Modern Life Makes It Hard to Be Happy,* proposed a set of modern norms as follows:

- Righteousness of Entitlement
- Rejection of Difficulty
- The Glamour of Potential
- The Assault on Detachment
- The Undermining of Responsibility
- A Loss of Transcendence

From an early age we develop a heavy reliance on carefully attending to and learning from other people, often using mentalizing skills and using cues such as success and prestige to figure out from whom to learn. The extent to how heavily we look to others above our own experience or intuition calibrates us for the world we encounter. We have evolved to become rapid learners of culture- it is the very secret of our species success.[102] People conform strongly to social behavioural norms. We tend to take cues for behaviour in most social contexts from the actions of others. This pressure is called the *conformity bias*. When deciding what to do, we look around and see what others most commonly do in this situation and imitate them. For good or bad, conformity bias is necessary for cumulative cultural development to take place. In peer pressured groups one is more conscious of the social cost, lest they become the nail that sticks up, the tall poppy. In many hapless classrooms, learners keep their heads down.

Dewey believed that *everything depends on the quality of experience which is had*.[103] Our situated experience changes, as we do. To this end consider the table on the next page which cross references each action skill to behaviour opportunities that may arise in different situations. The behaviour conditioning skills of Attention, Appreciation, Ability, and Authorship might develop over time and work with each other to support cultural learning outcomes that are specific, measurable and meaningful. The affective responses of Openness, Otherness, Personal Ownership and Optimism (in engaging with challenge) arise culturally as beneficial outcomes.

Questions of meaning and identity can be addressed in a fresh and original manner, by viewing action as a mode for human togetherness. Positive culture evolves from the shared participation in worthy causes. The more one does good, the more it becomes part of their self-image and to become one who condones good (just as the opposite is true). Self-perception is a core feedback loop for the dynamic emergence of personal qualities over time. As demonstrated with the successful Positive Action programme discussed earlier in "Context for Action".

Positive Behaviours from the Action Skillset

	Bring to Attention	Liberate Ability
Generate Appreciation	Openness, Pluralism	Otherness, Altruism
Provide Authorship	Ownership, Responsibility	Engagement, Optimism

One of the most original contributors to twentieth century political thought, Hannah Arendt, warns us against a conception (and practice) of education that simply focuses on the transmission of knowledge from teacher to students, without with opportunities for 'grasping' the world and understanding it. In having a capacity to forgive, the capacity to keep one's word, we find freedoms. We have freedom to undo and renew though forgiveness. We will cope better with a world of uncertainty through the security of trustworthiness.

Tony Little, former headmaster at Eton in his book, An Intelligent Person's Guide to Education,[104] reminds us: *"We will continue to have our measurement and statistics and we will continue to scrutinise and applaud intellectual achievement but we must give at least equal weight to the qualities on which success and happiness will depend, the flexibility and capacity to deal with uncertainty, the confidence to drive change and an acute awareness of the connectedness of things, all expressed through a tolerant humanity."*

Celebrating shared purpose, connecting meaningful experiences to the narrative- helps students to better interpret a positive school story for themselves. To a school leader without the aura of legacy and "hallowed halls", this all might sound fanciful– however such confidence in community and courage to be bold is needed from leadership. For just as culture is cumulative and evolving, it is made so by comparative associations – without momentum or a hopeful stand to make, you will be drawn down to the melée.

Let's capture the right behaviours and provide the opportunity to share publicly. Whilst the discipline of the school must reflect that of life it must do so wisely. The pioneer Sociologist Emile Durkheim warned that *"when accolades are used primarily for stimulating the qualities of intelligence, rather than those of the heart, success rather than moral merit... then those ranks, prizes and honours are reserved only for the most intelligent students rather than the most upright and sensitive consciousness... there is reason to believe that prestige may attach too exclusively, in school life, to intellectual merit, and that a greater share should be accorded moral value. To do this it is not necessary to add new tests ...or to add new prizes to our list of honours. It would be enough for the teacher to attach more importance to those qualities that in current practice, evidently are too often treated as a secondary thing. The affection and friendship that he evidences for the hardworking student, whose efforts do not bring the same success ... would be by itself the best rewards and would restore a balance."* [105]

We should challenge that which makes little or no direct connection between the pupils' context and purposes. The approach needed is one sensitive to the context and bespoke in its ability to account for cultural, regional, historical, and socio-economic backgrounds. Beware static off-the-shelf offerings- each intervention should be as unique as the participants and the meaning they attribute to the experience. In appreciating the importance of connectivity, we should provide situations that elicit the best behaviours, more relevant learning and support a legacy for the school culture - that is the Awe in Action this book attends to.

If it is through *the doing* that we gain experiences, it is through *reflecting* we create meanings. In reflection and story-telling we support connection as the child *stitches their knowledge to their experiences.* It is through the personal reflection and sharing that magic moments begin to form – they are woven into personal narratives and identity. In sharing stories of awe, we relive and recolour our narrative and in adjustment, we redraft our self-concept to better serve us in a complex and unpredictable world. We need to allow time and space for this to shape in pupils' minds. In this way the situation offered through an outdoor adventurous experience may be a powerful opportunity for supporting the development of positive concept and addressing values in school.

School of Hard Knocks
By Jon Spears

The Social Mobility Commission's 2017 report[106], 'State of the Nation', makes for stark reading for schools like ours. Sitting at the heart of Tamworth, a 'cold spot' for social mobility and the 26th worst area for school indicators in the country, the commission has confirmed what we have known for some time- all of the odds are stacked against us.

The social inequality of our local community is something that keeps me awake at night; it drives me on and makes me hide in abject terror in equal measures. I grew up in the community I now serve, I went to the school in which I now teach; I know these people, their struggles and the depths to which they must reach to awaken that modicum of human spirit that enables us to stand tall, find that fight and rise above the imposed barriers and bricks that our postcode can bring.

My working day consists of constantly battling to alleviate the myriad of socio-economic factors that threaten to derail even the smallest slice of success experienced by our disadvantaged students. It is a job that entails swimming against the tide, batting obstacle after obstacle aside and regularly relying on that most British of reserves: sheer bloody determination, just to get through the day. Is it any wonder that 70% of teachers in schools such as ours are more likely to leave the profession?

The report does offer some hope though, after all if London, with its appalling levels of deprivation and inequality, can buck the national trend of schools failing to close the gaps between the disadvantaged and their more advantaged peers, then there is surely

115

a chance for all of us. There is clear evidence being presented by the Commission that the collaborative initiatives and extra funding being pumped into London schools has benefitted the lives of young people. It is also apparent that multi-cultural schools do better in terms of closing the gap; it seems the cultural impact on parenting, which places great value on education and ambition, is giving a huge step-up to offspring that our white, working (or unemployed) communities just can't manage. There is a good argument that pupil premium funding would be better spent directly on families, enabling them to access, appreciate and accelerate the chances of a better life that schooling can offer.

Culture can represent a huge chasm between the disadvantaged and their advantaged peers and it is often overlooked in the exploration of underachievement in schools. Students who, from a young age, are learning to play instruments, appreciate art and literature, understand the impact of history and politics in their lives have a much greater chance of being that articulate, thoughtful, intelligent, well-rounded candidate we all look for at interviews. These are the students most likely to get those best University places and professional jobs. Whilst many London students cannot afford home tuition, or do not have parents promoting these cultural jewels, London schools do have a wealth of opportunities to access cultural activities and learning on their doorstep and are clearly using them. Obviously, that is not to say that those of us in market towns have no access to such opals- Tamworth has a rich history to mine- but with a community who not only undervalue, but actively fight against their children developing a love of arts and humanities, the battle appears futile. We have parents who refuse to allow their children to learn about the Muslim faith, the only exposure to the arts is the weekly viewing of the X-Factor and, as for politics, two students recently went on their first visit to London, to participate in a Britain First rally. For so many of our students it is much easier for them to believe they have a chance of being a celebrity than a medic or barrister, after all, they see more people like them on the TV than they do in the stuffy establishments they try to avoid at all costs.

The factors that have led to these societal divides and breakdowns have not gone away under the successive governments during my lifetime, indeed they have gotten worse. We have nurses, teachers and other professionals now using services once the sole reserve of the unemployed; I know many people struggling (and feeling deep shame as a result) whose Christmas presents this year have been purchased from car boot sales and charity shops.

Clearly the challenge goes way beyond secondary schools and their use of Pupil Premium funding. No matter how much we close gaps within school, and we are slowly beginning to close the gaps, we cannot begin to tap into the wider aspects that need to dramatically change in order to level the playing field. Our disadvantaged cohort have had six years of education, twelve years of life, by the time they join us. Their underachievement, lack of aspiration and sense of self-worth are as well established as the poverty in which they have grown up. We receive extra funding for these students and have to evidence how this funding has cured a lifetime of social neglect; the reality is that the money is used to keep most schools afloat themselves. Schools that can't recruit the outstanding subject specialist but have to rely on unqualified teachers or supply staff; schools that are now on their fourth consecutive year of redundancies, allowing support staff and teaching assistants to shrink away into oblivion. In hitting schools like ours with reduced funding, despite pushing schools to better support the disadvantaged in deprived areas, the government has unwittingly created a raft of schools that truly mirror their communities, rather than offering a way out. Once a beacon of light during dark times, they are becoming a new breed of impoverished, underachievers- unable to recruit or retain staff and unable to move out of the 'requires improvement' or 'special measures' categories designed, it seems, to keep schools like ours in our place.

And yet we fight on. There are days I am overwhelmed by the poverty, neglect, despair and bleakness of the future for some of our youngsters, but I have to believe that I can make a difference, that there is a way out and that things will change. After all I am living proof that the shackles placed upon you, due to the area you live, need not define you. You can succeed despite growing up with financial and cultural inequality. All we can do is focus on the things that we know are having an impact on our young people's lives and keep fighting for them.

MASTERY, MOUNTAINS &
MATHEMATICS

"...it can be considered that no one can experience elation who has never known despair; no one can be courageous without having known fear. So, the human personality... can be brought into flower by enhancing experiences" Earl C. Kelly 1962, The Fully Functioning Self, p18.

Some fear the peaks and live in their shadow. Some choose to climb. The metaphor of the mountain in learning can help in our understanding and perhaps illuminate the benefits of a different approach. Snowy alpine peaks can be an intimidating prospect. Impossibly looming at times, there is a sense they are menacing and untouchable. Yet the sense of novelty and adventure also draws out an inner temptation. It is not until one loses themselves in the busyness of training and climbing that they see how close the summits can be. One's active efforts can create both courage and reward.

The aim of the inaccessible mountain top is essential to the endeavour of mountaineering, but in-itself, not sufficient. Something else is being achieved through the experience - the becoming of a mountaineer. At the summit, climbers from the Tyrolean region of northern Italy give a greeting of "Bergheil"– a simple mountain greeting of congratulations for the summit, a salute to being there and importantly a wish for wellbeing and future success. It is the doing of mountaineering that is being celebrated here and not just a result of completing a challenge. The best of thoughts, intentions and resolutions come to nothing unless employed. It is the continuation of the journey that counts.

The spirit of this greeting is what we should wish for the students of Mathematics – that they would see the learning of maths about becoming Mathematicians, searching out interesting and beautiful challenges to attempt. Perhaps too they could celebrate success with a wish for wellbeing and more good challenges to come. Like the Mountaineer, a Mathematician is not solely concerned with finding solutions but also in seeking new problems too.

So much fortune is lost on rejected hopes, passive wishes and plied fears. The comfort zone will always beckon us. Yet a full life is not for the spectator – action is life itself. Those discouraged students become seekers of safety and are apt to disengage and become passive on-lookers. And why wouldn't they, just look at the conditioning that happens through the process of schooling.

We begin to label children with signs of their potential at an early age. Well before they start secondary school, children are streamlined into ability groupings -an approach broadly unchanged since the 1950's. The traditional British concern with ensuring some of our ablest students reach the highest possible standards has resulted in a "lose-lose" situation. In secondary schools, the "Top Set" classes are overcrowded and the label of "Bottom Set" gives some an excuse to avoid difficulty. In class, curriculum time has become sacrosanct with school leaders pressurised for fast solutions to the chronic problems that the political system they are part of has inexorably created.

If there is one subject that symbolises the great opportunity cost to learning more than any other, it is the teaching of Mathematics. This is a subject in which, at the time of writing, the majority of students achieve well below their potential. The facts are stark. Whilst at secondary school, a child spends approximately six hundred hours of class instruction in mathematics and similarly for English between the ages of 11 and 16. Despite this, in 2013 over 35% of children in the UK leave school without achieving a pass in both English and Maths and this figure persists. At the time of writing there are more than 250,000 people who leave each year without a pass grade in Maths or English and nine out of ten of them don't achieve any higher grade by the time they leave compulsory education at eighteen. Schools invest vast amounts on additional hours of tuition for the students who are falling in their studies. Despite research showing more instruction time does not help reducing the proportion of low-achieving students we keep on doing the same thing expecting different results. It takes courage to break from tradition, to look beyond short-term improvements. Too many school leaders feel they can see the child through the statistics. As per the well-known analogy, weighing the pig does not make it any heavier.

Our modern schooling is now expected to be accountable for the general malaise of adolescence. Too many children have a school experience in which they don't feel any responsibility. Too many leave school with a poor social capacity and a feeling of disenfranchisement. This is particularly so with the most socially disadvantaged populations. There is an overwhelming a need to directly challenge this. Like the farmer weighing his pig, if we approach the task in the same manner the results will not be much different. Enabling students to take ownership of their learning will.

We can better see the child through personally knowing them. Education does not lend itself to economies of scale. Growing children requires smaller class sizes, long term staff retention, pastoral development, shared service and achievement...yes whole child education is expensive but so too is reducing children to production units who are processed but purposeless. We should challenge any schooling culture which pushes a narrow exam focus alone –particularly for students aged between 15-18 years. We need to be creating sustainable individuals who can continually develop, contribute and engage their cultural literacy as they grow into the next adult generation of society.

The emphasis on a narrow inflexible 'compartmentalised' approach remains, in which it is often difficult to promote values for education and society as a whole (Keighley 1991 1996, Humberstone 1989 1993). What is disappointing is that this fact is so well known. The UK government invested in The Rose Report in 2008 which pointed the current shortcomings in the State primary school system then promptly swept aside its principal research findings. The Every Child Matters agenda introduced by the Children Act 2004; the statement of values by the National Forum for Values in Education and the Community have similarly been overlooked. The measures highlighted the importance of self, relationships, our society, and the environment. They were distilled into three aims for secondary education, enabling all children to become:

- Successful learners who enjoy learning, make progress and achieve;
- Confident individuals who are able to live safe, healthy and fulfilling lives;
- Responsible citizens who make a positive contribution to society.

Like the mountains, the subjects we teach are essential but, in themselves, not sufficient. As the mountaineer salutes to the challenge we should too - that same wish for wellbeing and success in the journey should be provided for. Just as the spirit of mountaineering is more than "summits", subjects like mathematics are more than solutions or knowledge. We can learn a lot more. Mathematics, like mountaineering is in the doing, rather than an end in itself. With the isolated difficulties of the mountains there is much kindness shown to fellow travellers. It brings out the best in us, why not then, in the classroom as children learn together in their journey towards mastery.

New Views- Wisdom from the Mountains

"Once when hiking up the north side of a Welsh mountain called Cader Idris I had a memorable learning experience. I had a group of nine girls of about thirteen years of age from inner city London. When the team had reached the saddle and made for the summit the students slowly began to succumb to doubt. Two girls, who had been moaning throughout the day, wore their colleagues down. They didn't want to be there and were protesting. When the team were perhaps an hour from the top it began to snow and the visibility reduced to about 10 metres. As the ascent grew harder a sense of defeatism set in. We carried on but more and more the team grew disheartened. At that time, I began to feel that reaching the summit would not be a reality. I began to fear that few of the students would grasp any meaning or value from our climb or the entire expedition - that the main reward of the day had been the summit view.

About 10 minutes from the top I asked the group to take a vote whether we pushed on for ten more minutes to the summit or if we just turned around there. Only four students wanted to continue. Despite my best efforts to encourage them onwards a impasse had been reached. We turned around and went down.

At that time, I felt I had made a big mistake especially as the weather cleared up as we began to descend. Later in the week, whilst working with the team on an environmental project, one of the girls who had protested the most mentioned that she now had wished she had gone to the top and she could now see reason... She had taken a lot away from the journey and saw a value from our climb. She regretted not pushing on and learned the value of persistence... I had thought that the main reward of the day had been the summit view... but it was something much deeper. She had found her spirit."

Courtesy of Janek Mamino, OB Senior Instructor.

SEEING DAYLIGHT

*One day Nasruddin entered his favourite teahouse and declared,
"The moon is more useful than the sun". When asked to explain
himself. Nasruddin replied, "Because we need the light more during
the night than during the day".*

Everyone seems an expert on education by the very fact
of their own schooling. We seek to prepare the child for life yet
cannot spare them from the classroom for exam grades.
Perhaps like Nasruddin, we see only the brightness of the
moon for what is missing. Sirens are sounding. Wise voices
such as Sir Ken Robinson[107] in his *"Changing education
paradigms"* makes clear a number of criticisms of the
contemporary education system – he argues it's failing too
many. Post industrialist school has parallels with the factory,
in the pursuit of output it inadvertently teaches children to be
passive, inert citizens. Radical thinkers such as Ivan Illich
would even question the view that we need schools. In
Deschooling Society, Illich suggested that we could learn, work
and transfer complex skills in a decentralised way, something
which is made possible with advances in technology and
online learning.[108] Still there is an inevitably in the repeated
cycle of educational policy. When I started writing this, there
was a return to the traditional transmission approach in
England. An approach which is associated with shallow
learning, summative assessment and final high stakes
examination. Four government Education Secretaries in four
years and we are seeing little attainment or progress from the

policy makers.§ The irony is not lost on the school leader.

At the heart of education is opportunity. The greatest dividend in education is opportunity gained, the greatest cost to education is when it is lost. Seems obvious, yet the pressures of austerity and the fickleness of policy has provided for a narrowed curriculum at best. A generation of opportunity lost at worst. The fleece has gone, exposing vulnerabilities- the value of health and wellbeing being most at risk. Consider opportunities lost in any given generation when parents feel that school is *something that just has to be done.* Those are hopes lost – the resultant low aspiration has a persistence -an intergenerational effect.

What is it we really teach children about the world? Has childhood merely become a rehearsal for a performance? Or per Shakespeare, a stage for just another *poor player*? To fit, to be pressed for productivity. Thousands of schools all offering the same outcomes and all competing for the highest attainment rates … a generic offering, in the main. Welcome to the educational "Hoover". It doesn't have to be this way. You will need courage for implementing the change needed. It was from similar sentiment and unfavourable personal experiences that the famous German Educationalist, Kurt Hahn was driven to change. Hahn believed that there had to be a purpose. The word *destiny* might not be spoken of openly, but it is in everyone's heart. The most effective curricula are those tailored to and developed with an active participant in mind.

---

§ Between 2014 and 2018 - *Michael Gove, Nicky Morgan, Justine Greening and Damien Hinds*

He did not dismiss the importance of examinations, but the *dimensionless emphasis* placed on them. The key to his participatory approach was instruction on the real (rather than imagined) issues relevant to each group; the only way to do this is through collaborative investigation and decision-making. There was in the learning, a greater expedition to be taken. To implement such an approach would not be an easy undertaking. It asked of the educator to question their role and the very purpose for education. Eventually a school followed where students would do things and take ownership of their learning; A school designed to help students discover their interests and passions, not just prepare them for tests. It would be a school where students would be engaged and motivated by understanding that their learning has relevance, meaning and purpose.

To make your way in life you need 3 things:
A deep sense of inner purpose and the will to renew it.
A clear vision of where you want to get to and the energy to pursue it.
And courage. Courage to take steps which others might fear to take.

Ralph Coverdale

Creating a Culture of Excellence
By Ron Berger, EL Education

"In carpentry there is no higher compliment builders give each other than this: That person is a craftsman. This one word says it all. It connotes someone who has integrity, knowledge, dedication, and pride in work—someone who thinks carefully and does things well. I want a classroom full of craftsmen – students whose work is strong, accurate, and beautiful; students who are proud of what they do and respect themselves and others."

Five Pedagogical Principles

1. *PURPOSE -Assign work that matters. Students need assignments that challenge and inspire them.*
2. *ASPIRE- Study examples of excellence. Before they begin work on a project, the teacher and students examine models of excellence – high-quality work done by previous students as well as work done by professionals.*
3. *COMMUNICATE -Build a culture of critique. Formal critique sessions build a culture of critique that is essential for improving students' work.: "Be kind; be specific; be helpful"*
4. *PERSIST -Require multiple revisions. In life, when the quality of one's work really matters, one almost never submits a first draft. An ethic of excellence requires revision.*
5. *SHARE- Provide opportunities for public presentation. Every final draft students complete is done for an outside audience – whether a class of kindergartners, the principal, or the wider community.*

OUR EMBODIED MIND

The world can only be grasped by action ... The hand is the cutting edge of the mind" - Jacob Bronowski

We all know that learning is necessarily a rich and complex journey that involves the whole-child – physically, emotionally and spiritually. Yet one could argue that the body has practically been banished from learning. It was Rene Descartes back in the mid seventeenth Century who could be held to account for the divorce of mind from matter- his conferring the mind with a special status[**], one which restricted it to a consciousness separate from any of the physical laws. Descartes' great influence in western thought popularised the idea of mind as some metaphysical higher gift for the next three centuries.

The term "Cartesian Catastrophe" coined by playwright Arthur Koestler, adequately sums up the consequence on western thinking. Descartes error led to *an impoverishment of psychology which it took three centuries to remedy even in part.* Though Psychology has now begun to readdress its over emphasis on the mind apart, the education policy makers have yet to become aware. The Cartesian Catastrophe has been yet more destructive. Cartesian Dualism encompasses a set of views – not just about the relationship between mind and matter- but also which implicitly prescribe a privilege

---

[**] *Influenced by a Platonic sense of the world, Descartes had argued for the separation of mind from material and hence the mind from the body. Referred to as "Cartesian Dualism"*

responsible for much human exploitation of, and destructiveness towards nature. A mind separated from material, is a mind separated from body- is a person separated from planet. This simple dualistic way of thinking sees the world in terms of polar-opposites and is an approach that conceptualises the world in a damaging human-centric way (anthropocentrism). Sadly, it seems education remains the last field to operate on Cartesian assumptions. The logic of policy makers implies that it doesn't really matter how the information gets in. Only the exam results matter.

The human body's innate structures such as its sense organs, muscles and brain require activity for health and growth. Their functional capacity demands us to move and interact. Our very nerve cells are not inert, rather than being passively aroused to action by primary drives (e.g. hunger, thirst, and pain), the cells of the brain are spontaneously active, even during sleep. All our cells are self-organising and with the high degree of interaction between the micro and macroscopic levels we become a product of our acts as much as our acts are the result our choices.

Human brains constantly monitor the incoming information from the five senses (sight, sound, touch, smell and taste) plus the information generated internally (regarding the state of the body and what is stored in memory). The brain decides what to do next at a rate of about one thousand times per second. Our basic drive is to make things happen, to explore, investigate, manipulate and come to terms with the environment. Phenomena such as curiosity and wonderment are primary and inherent.

Like any other animal ours was a bodily development. Just as Darwin showed for the Cross-Bill Finch, we too resulted from countless selections in response to the interaction with the environment. Homo Saipan became from fitness; not bestowed by divine selection[109]. According to Bjorn Merker, it was mobility itself that created the need to develop a "work space"- neural networks. The brain necessarily developed to accommodate for the special kinds of decision making associated with mobility. Whereas the vascular systems of plants are sufficient for the more limited range of circumstances to which they require a response from. Mobile living systems have such a large variety of potential choices that they cannot possibly rely on genetic endowment alone; they must have the capacity to learn quickly to deal with the kinds of new situations into which their mobility thrusts them. Hence the brain evolved, not to think or feel, but to control movement. In the book *"Consciousness Explained,"* Daniel C. Dennett uses the life of a sea squirt as an example in case:

"The juvenile sea squirt wanders through the sea searching for a suitable rock or chunk of coral to cling to and make it home for life. For this task, it has a rudimentary nervous system. When it finds its spot and takes root, it doesn't need its brain anymore, so it eats it!" (page 177)

Of all the examples used to illustrate the physical cause of the mind, none is more striking that the well-known case of that Phineas Gage. In 1848 Phineas was shockingly injured in an explosion whilst preparing a blast hole on a railway construction site. He suffered destruction of his frontal lobes from a projectile iron rod that shot through his left cheek and out the top of his skull. He survived yet his brain trauma resulted in radical personality changes. The damage to his frontal cortex resulted in a loss of social inhibitions. The once charming gentleman became "fitful, irreverent, indulging at times in the grossest profanity". The physical destruction of part of Phineas' brain, caused drastic changes in his mind. Neuroscientists have subsequently shown a causal relation between damage to the brain and mental deterioration. Today we know that every time the brain is injured, the mind is also injured. It is clear that body and mind are tightly connected.

The importance of bodily movement for the brain is encapsulated in Dennett's story of the Sea Squirt. Here the brain's physical existence evolved solely from a need for movement. Recent research shows how the body is an important part of the learning process. Studies provide evidence that increased aerobic fitness levels correlate with enhanced cognitive and brain plasticity[110] and that that aerobic exercise can improve a number of aspects of cognition and performance- outcomes related to scholastic achievement. In addition, when we read, we tend to activate the same sensory and motor brain areas involved in doing what we are reading about. When people make small body movements in the fMRI scanner, say moving their feet, fingers, or tongue, they activate regions in the sensory and motor cortex involved in moving these body parts. Most interesting, when people read words associated with the leg, mouth, and arm ("kick," "pick" and "lick"), they activate these same sensory motor brain areas.

Both moving your foot and understanding the world "kick" are governed by similar areas of the motor cortex. It's hard to separate the reading mind from the doing one.

Few have had more of an impact on the thinking of the body's primacy in consciousness than that of the French philosopher Merleau-Ponty. He influentially underlined the fact that there is an inherent consciousness in and out of the body - a *corporeity of consciousness.*[††] He recognized that one's own body is not only a thing but is also a permanent condition of experience. More recently influential thinkers such as Shaun Gallaher and prominent neuroscientists,[111] have argued that "our awareness of reality doesn't depend entirely on what is happening inside the brain, but a side effect of how we, as individuals interact with the world." Their main hypothesis is that mind, body, and world mutually interact and influence one another. Gallagher claims that the body shapes the mind at a fundamental basic level, even if it remains "behind the scene" (p. 141). Our consciousness requires the joint operation of the brain, body and world. Who we are and what we know are inseparable from where we are and what we are doing. Consciousness arises from interactions with our surroundings:

Action also means health. The psychobiological approach is generating evidence that suggests the association of exercise with psychological wellbeing and mental health is just as convincing as exercise and physical health. In the final analysis one cannot separate physical health from mental

---

[††]*In the Phenomenology of Perception Merleau-Ponty wrote: "Insofar as I have hands, feet; a body, I sustain around me intentions which are not dependent on my decisions and which affect my surroundings in a way that I do not choose" (1962, p. 440). "*

health. What you think can impact your body. This mind-body connection is called *psychosomatic*. The effects of chronic mental stress leading to digestive and/or bowel distress is a common example. What may be even more important and perhaps more impactful to your health is the converse relationship called *somatopsychic*, the body-mind relationship or when the condition of the body affects the mind. Physiological health and function is apparent through alterations in wellbeing, sleep, appetite, motivation, energy level, body experience and function. It is impossible to separate the body from the mind- so closely interwoven and complex the relationship, we continue to make new discoveries to this day.

Clearly all learning is embodied, it is situated and is discursive at some level. Knowledge and learning emerge, develop and are adapted in the process of participating in activity (Fenwick 2001). It might seem obvious to say that "Learning is not done in a vacuum" and yet in actual practice, this is the basis of what many educationalists operate on.

Lesson plans are designed with the sea squirt in mind, as if the body is unnecessary, with students permanently affixed to their desks.

Ask and you will be told by many that there is not enough curriculum time for learning outside the classroom. Yet the holistic nature of learning is well recognised - policy has even legislated for addressing the whole child. It is the structure of our schooling systems and the short term competitive performance priorities that have prevented this from being practically the case. We might return to the beginning and ask again "What *is* education for?" Are we simply processing children for employment? Are the priorities of state education a form of indentured labour? For whatever answer you find, recognise the holistic nature of learning and challenge the assumption of the mind's autonomy from the body. Philosophers may interpret the world in different ways; the point is to change it, indeed to better it.

The fact is that all experiences are mediated through our bodies. People, place, activity and culture are constituents of any experience. It seems obvious to say that our brain is host to our mind and yet we overlook the wellbeing of the body that is host. Every nerve in our body restlessly seeks stimulus. Just being is doing. *I exist therefore I think*. We are not human beings so much as human doings!

"To learn to think we must [move] exercise our limbs, our senses and our bodily organs which are the tools of intellect. ...it is a good bodily constitution that makes the workings of the mind easy and correct."
(Rousseau from Emile, Treatise on Education", 1762)

ACTION LEARNING

"Give the pupils something to do, not something to learn; and the doing is of such a nature as to demand thinking; learning naturally results" J. Dewey, Democracy and Education Ch 12

We cannot but learn – it is our very nature- and we learn from the context of learning as much as the content. Take the traditional approach to education as an example, with its emphasis on rote memory and exam-based performance it pushes students to approach learning on a shallow surface level, to develop superficial strategies, and have performance, rather than mastery or intrinsic motivation. It has been shown that attitudes to learning can account for as much as 30% of performance. Academic achievement is in fact mediated by a learners' ideas of learning; according to (Biggs, 1987; Marton and Saljo, 1997), students develop either:

- a *superficial level* of understanding (surface approach to learning, *where students are extrinsically motivated to care about details* to be reproduced later, using repetitive strategies),
- or a *deep approach* to learning (where students *are intrinsically motivated* to focus on the main ideas, using meaning-based strategies),
- or an *achievement approach* motivated by the need to achieve deep connections/ understanding

The point here is that the assessment framework dictates the relationship students have with their learning and accordingly the mindset that will follow. It is shocking that the development of fixed mind-sets and poor attitudes to learning can be directly attributed to the school's choice of delivery and assessment. It impacts values in education and the extent to which it prioritises performance over development. Those students who are most able are better able to adapt the epistemological beliefs and remain engaged with learning, whilst the less able student develops limiting beliefs and a shallow approach to education which discourages them for life.

The notion of Action Learning is a deceptively simple approach to human development in which small groups learn from each other's failures and victories rather than from "expert" instruction. It shouldn't be confused with activity for busyness sake.

Action Learning is a carefully structured strategy pioneered by Reg Revans. The approach based on his personal experiences during the war in the mines- he saw what values and goodness arises from of "comrades in adversity". Thinking about this at the coal board, and in the NHS, Revans was struck by the potential released by the ability to own up to ignorance without fear of ridicule or reprisal, and the inability of traditional "chalk and talk" teaching methods to solve practical problems or provide a framework for real human growth. His principles come down to *"teaching little and learning a lot"*.

The 1970's was a time of great upheaval and the

management wisdom of Revans and others played a significant part in the development of corporate competitiveness at the time. Indeed "Revans' Law" states *that for an organisation to survive, its rate of learning must be at least equal to the rate of change in its external environment*. But learning is hard.

Consultants such as John Adair and Ralph Coverdale were some of the other pioneers at the time. They developed short courses involving Simulated Learning projects delivered as structured exercises that allow students to practice team leadership in a changing environment and with innovative goals. This structure provided a period where management training blossomed. Outdoor management courses soon became popular too, aiming at improving members' understanding of team building and team leadership by group problem solving in outdoor situations. These short term 'Study-groups' offered leaderless group experiences in which members, with the aid of a 'facilitator', could review and reassess their behaviour as team members. The predominant approach was to use short courses and simulated projects.

By contrast, with his Action Learning approach, Revan's sought for the teams to work over *sustained periods* on significant *real-life problems*, with tutorial assistance, typically conducted in a new organisational surrounding. The work was prone to diversifying in many directions and introducing discovery methods alongside the more traditional lecture and syndicate discussion methods.

What Coverdale, Adair and Revan's had in common in their approach was the concept of inductive learning, as opposed to traditional deductive learning. They each helped in building ways of deeper thinking and better ways of working, (for example with generalising to produce a principle or way of behaving from observation). This is invaluable for students. Such collaborative behaviour interventions involve Metacognition, Self-regulation, Socio-emotional learning, all of which have been identified by the Education Endowment Foundation as the most secure forms of improving performance (by up to five months of teaching time).

Today there exists a framework for comprehensive school improvement that uses a similar philosophy and pedagogy to make learning more hands-on, project-based, and adventurous. A range of successful approaches[112] have rolled out across many charter schools in the USA. The expeditionary learning approach is strengthening and expanding overseas. Take for example the growth of EL Education which was born out of a collaboration between The Harvard Graduate School of Education and Outward Bound USA in the 1990's. Today they have over 150 schools across 30 states and have the support of rigorous independent research. This approach is no longer an outlier and is challenging the given educational traditionalists on their own home ground- academic results. The changes at schools that fully implement the Expeditionary Learning programme of EL Education extend beyond academics.[113] Student attendance improves; teacher retention and attendance improves; disciplinary problems go down, finding success in discipline, attendance, as well as with the academic domain.

Kurt Hahn's vision and rationale for childhood learning provide for a structure of learning that brings out the best in children, developing skills, qualities of character, resilience and a lifelong love of learning. To those who are leading the implementation of expeditionary learning strategies, this purpose and value is as obvious as daylight.

"they feel like activists because they are activists" - Cheryl Dobbertin

Realising Potential
By Hollie Jones, Joseph Leckie Academy

"Many students I work with are disaffected and disengaged at worst and at best quietly apathetic so as I stood beaming from the front of the assembly hall, excitedly promoting the benefits of joining TED-Ed Club to year 9; the empowerment, instilling of confidence, and the platform to share their brilliance. I should have perhaps been less surprised than I was to see a sea of blank faces looking back at me. I should have also been less surprised at the lack of initial interest. After a week or so I had had about four students come to me expressing a mild interest, not enough to commit to joining, but happy to take a letter and think about it. Evidently these students had not been won over by me and my overbearing enthusiasm so I did what any respectable teacher would do and set about coercing them into joining,

The first meeting of TED-Ed Club members commenced, after October half term. I stressed again the principles of the programme

and the background of the TED organisation. Some students looked confused, some looked a little sceptical and the chorus of questions that followed revolved around "What's in it for me? What do we get for doing this? Do I have to come every week?" Concerned that the point of this had escaped them I changed tack completely. I explained that the first stage in this programme was developing our character through social action. I decided to be clear and very blunt with them, to emphasise how important this aspect was. I told them quite clearly that in every class, that every one of them attended I could almost guarantee that there were students in there suffering from first world poverty. I told them that some of their classmates ate just once a day, and that was at school, due a lack of money at home. I told them that out of the hundreds of students they pass in the corridor every day, a select number of them would go home tonight to a house with very little inside. I then showed them a headline which stated that Walsall was one of the worst places in the entirety of the UK to live for safety, aspiration, comfort and a sense of belonging and identity. What I had said shocked them into silence. I wasn't expecting what happened next. Every student in the room began turning to each other and talking earnestly and excitedly. Suggestions came flooding in on how to change things for our school but also their community. They asked "Miss, what can we do?" and I told them "it's up to you, what do you feel you could do?" In the next 30 minutes I witnessed a buzz, an energy and a fervent dialogue the likes of which I've never before in a lesson. The students grabbed markers from my desk and covered my whiteboard, electronic screen, sugar paper and dozens of post it notes in ideas for fundraisers, awareness raising, volunteering and opportunities for community collaboration. From Christmas hamper drives to stories and Christmas carols at local hospices, nurseries and *care homes to sponsored staff vs student sports days and Big brother/ sister mentoring programmes, the ideas just kept coming. When the hour was up, I told them they were free to go. They stayed for another 30 minutes and organised amongst themselves to come back the following afternoon after school. Then the following lunchtime. And the lunchtime after that. They asked if they could contribute their own money, and if their families would be allowed to donate food and decorations. I was blown away by their generosity of time, spirit and resources. Using their vision, determination and consistent effort these students have mobilised in a way I've never seen before.*

As the programme continues and we look deeper at how best we can develop our character and personal leadership skills, I am excited to see in which direction these students will channel their energies, and how they will put the theory into practice through acting in service."

Courtesy of Character Matters Journal Dec. 2017.

Ten Expeditionary Learning Principles

Expeditionary Learning is built on ten design principles that reflect the educational values and beliefs of Kurt Hahn, founder of The Outward Bound Trust. These Ten principles seek to describe a caring, school culture and support an adventurous approach to learning:

1. The primacy of self-discovery:

Learning happens best with emotion, challenge and the requisite support. People discover their abilities, values, passions, and responsibilities in situations that offer adventure and the unexpected. Students undertake tasks that require perseverance, fitness, craftsmanship, imagination, self-discipline, and significant achievement. The teacher's primary task is to help students overcome their fears and discover they can do more than they think they can.

2. The having of wonderful ideas:

Teaching fosters curiosity about the world by creating learning situations that provide something important to think about, time to experiment, and time to make sense of what is observed.

3. The responsibility for learning:

Learning is both a personal process of discovery and a social activity. Everyone learns both individually and as part of a group. Every aspect of an Expeditionary Learning school encourages both children and adults to become increasingly responsible for directing their own personal and collective learning.

4. Empathy and caring:

Learning is fostered best in communities where students' and teachers' ideas are respected and where there is mutual trust. Learning groups are small in Expeditionary Learning schools, with a caring adult looking after the progress and acting as an advocate for each child. Older students mentor younger ones, and students feel physically and emotionally safe.

5. Success and failure:

All students need to be successful if they are to build the confidence and capacity to take risks and meet increasingly difficult challenges. But it is also important for students to learn from their failures, to persevere when things are hard, and to learn to turn disabilities into opportunities.

6. Collaboration and competition:

Individual development and group development are integrated so that the value of friendship, trust, and group action is clear. Students are encouraged to compete not against each other but with their own personal best and with rigorous standards of excellence.

7. Diversity and inclusion:

Both diversity and inclusion increase the richness of ideas, creative power, problem-solving ability, respect for others. In Expeditionary Learning schools, students investigate the value their different histories and talents as well as those of other cultures.

8. The natural world:

Direct respectful relationship with the natural world refreshes the human spirit teaches the important ideas of recurring cycles and cause and effect. Students learn to become stewards of the earth and of future generations.

9. Solitude and reflection:

Students and teachers need time alone to explore their own thoughts, make their own connections, and create their own ideas. They also need time to exchange their reflections with others.

10. Service and compassion:

We are crew, not passengers. Students and teachers are strengthened by acts of consequential service to others and a sense of collective responsibility.

IMPELLED THROUGH ADVENTURE AND CHALLENGE

"Our Muscular vigour ...will always be needed to furnish the background of sanity, serenity and cheerfulness to life, to give moral elasticity to our disposition, to round off the wiry edge of our fretfulness, and make us good humoured."
William James: 1899 p.207

Enhancing student engagement and decreasing apathy through adventure-based education has its roots with Kurt Hahn, who in 1941, together with Lawrence Holt, developed The Outward Bound Sea School and developed is programme towards addressing student disaffection. Outward Bound placed students in active, adventure-based situations, subscribing to the notion that students who learned to engage successfully and surmount physical challenges could do the same with emotional, academic, and moral challenges.[114]

Recent scholars have called for the use of active pedagogies to help college students engage more fully in the academic experience.[115] An adventure-based class represents an active pedagogy that can support the goals of a school curriculum: getting to know peers, learning critical thinking skills, and learning about wellbeing and benefits from virtuous behaviours. As researchers report trends in students becoming increasingly disengaged,[116] more powerful and intense engagement experiences may be necessary if students are to receive the maximum social and educational benefits from college. The use of an adventure-based pedagogy demonstrates promise in providing students with an impactful learning environment. The practical nature of these experiences supports better judgement. From virtues in action comes practical wisdom (Phronesis) to inform behaviour with an ethic of service (Praxis) that leads the student towards a way of being which finds purpose and a flourishing life.

According to the idea central to Outward Bound, physical challenges can teach students how to overcome challenges in other areas, whether academic, ethical, or social.[117] The process of meeting a challenging condition and being able to successfully manage it provides an important lesson and feedback in how to succeed. The physical activities can be used as metaphors to other challenging processes, the adventure experience provide a way to practice overcoming challenges in different environments. [118]

BUILDING RESILIENCE

We would be doing a disservice to our young if we do not prepare them for the for a competitive and challenging world they will live in. Stress is a part of life that is unavoidable. We need a certain a level of stress to perform at our best. High Stakes examinations remain an important part of the learning process.[119]

The pursuit of high standards and deadlines are challenges that continue throughout life. What is needed is training through experience. Yet, the idea of preparing children for high stakes test by giving them more high stakes tests and at younger ages, misses the point completely.

Young people should be exposed to scenarios of challenge and adventure in big environments in order to draw out resilience and inoculate against stress. The challenge that a course at The Outward Bound Trust offers is just this. The qualities of resilience, selflessness, initiative and discipline are the skills for life which must be acquired through repeated experience. Such skills cannot be taught from a book. They must be lived. Through explicit training comes the refinement of skills that can unlock potential.

Wilderness settings support mental health and wellbeing[120], they can be very effective experiences for using transactional strategies that draw out learning and positive responses.[121] They can be very effective in addressing learned helplessness and self-limiting behaviours.

Just as a medic or a firefighter is trained to act through difficult and dangerous experiences, we too can develop a resilience through exposure to *inoculating experiences*. The Transactional model of stress and coping is a way to understand how people deal with challenge and their emotions during a difficult or threatening experience. Within the transactional model, coping behaviours can be viewed as the result of on-going transactions among personal and environmental factors, perceptions of threat or stress, and the perceived effectiveness of coping strategies. In facilitating scenarios that expose us to challenge and higher levels of stress (e.g. as winter expeditions or scrambling in a wet gorge) we will more likely take up direct action through changing the environmental conditions and by doing so adopt vital skills.[122]

EXERCISE AND EXPERIENCE

*The mind strives to imagine only those things which posit its power
of acting.* – Spinoza

The bodily effect of exercise on one's brain can have an important impact on our perception (mood or elevation), and how we draw on imagination and bring on episodic memory. We engage in the world differently for that moment. Physical action influences our receptiveness to experiences. Is there a serotonin switch? or a Dopamine dial? a Hippocampal gear-housing? [123] Yes. Exercise has a profound effect on our brain chemistry, physiology and neuroplasticity. It affects not only our ability to think, create and solve, but also our mood and our ability to *lean into uncertainty,* risk, judgement and anxiety in a substantial measurable way.

Exercise may be the simple most important method of enhancing those aspects of children's mental functioning that are central to cognitive and social development. The condition of the body clearly affects the mind - known as a *somatopsychic* effects. Even relatively low levels of physical activity can enhance our sense of wellbeing. The benefits may not just be to our bodily functions but to our emotional need for belonging and connection.

The body has been somehow banished from learning, along with the body's enmeshments in its social, material and cultural nets of action. Then, appropriated by both school and workplace, the learning that is harvested from bodies in action has been forced into normalizing categories, commodified, and credentialed. [124]

Professor Stuart Biddle of Loughborough University, a specialist on motivation and sport, argues that the 'feel good' effect of physical activity has great potential for our wellbeing and mental health. His book *Physical Activity and Psychological Wellbeing* provides research demonstrating the relationship between physical exercise and mental health, including exercise. He shows how exercise has an impact on anxiety, depression, mood and emotion, self-esteem and cognitive functioning

Physical activity doesn't just build muscle and stronger hearts. Through the release of feel-good hormones and enhanced connections with other people being physically active does wonders for our wellbeing and wellbeing leads to success. Research has shown:

- Healthy active students get better results
- Physical activity leads to better mood and positive emotions
- Positive mood influences memory choices/reflective self.
- Active learning leads to better recall.
- Healthy diet choices support students' learning.

We can choose how we feel. we have a choice about our biology.[125] Yet, statistics from the most recent large-scale childhood obesity survey in the UK reveal that 25 percent of boys and 33 percent of girls aged between two and nineteen years are overweight or obese. Recent research on physical activity in Scotland found that there are three times as many inactive children as there are active. Despite influential researchers advising on the importance of activity, recess is being sacrificed for more academic time in the classroom and organised inter-school sport ends when students are just 16 years old in the English state school system. Examples as Howard Gardner, author of *Frames of Mind*- who argues for the importance nurturing our bodily kinaesthetic intelligence as one of his eight Multiple Intelligences. Another important voice is John Raty (2008) author of *Spark: The revolutionary new science of exercise on the brain* which argues that exercise changes the expression of fear and anxiety, as well as the way the brain processes experiences. Raty points to a number of proven chemical pathways which, with the brain's neuro-plastic abilities, act to cause changes to the brains processing. We are continually changing our brains by the way we are using them.

Learning and knowledge are not independent substances to be consumed, rather they emerge, develop and are adapted in the process of participation in the activity (Fenwick, 2001) Recognising the importance of the 'holistic' nature of learning (people, place, activity, culture) and the need for activity is thus crucial. We must be more sympathetic to the struggles and tensions of everyday life.

Per Spinoza: *"a body more capable ... of doing things at once or being acted on in many ways at once so its mind is more capable ...of perceiving many things at once ". "Self Esteem is a joy born of the fact that man considers himself and his powers of acting".* [126] It is the quality of our action that gives personal reflection its very character and significance.

ACTING TO CONSERVE

"Acts of creation are ordinarily reserved for gods and poets, but humbler folk may circumvent this restriction if they know how. To plant a pine, for example, one need be neither god nor poet; one need only own a good shovel." - Aldo Leopold
Pines Above the Snow, A Sand County Almanac.

There are many opportunities afforded by the outdoor environment that support authentic, purposeful, real life tasks. Experience in nature is so important in teaching people to be more resourceful and more grounded in themselves. The rich, sensory setting of a natural place greatly stimulates children's own investigations and provides an ideal context for group activities in which the development of capacities and skills can occur. Risk-taking in natural environments has been linked to positive development of children's learning paths and dispositions. Similarly, the potential for children to develop both a confidence in themselves and the disposition to manage risk effectively has been linked to young children's physical risk-taking in the outdoor environment. Yet research suggests that school teachers miss many of the opportunities afforded by the outdoor environment with which to enhance children's learning. It appeared that playing in the outdoor environment was seen as having little to do with what teachers saw as their primary role: that of 'teaching' curriculum content. Observation data indicated that the teachers' 'normal' outdoor learning sessions allowed little more freedom than that of the classroom.

Hahn believed nature teaches us necessity, "working in an environment you cannot predict produces challenges and weather and darkness before you're ready for darkness". Experience in nature is so important in teaching people to be more resourceful and more grounded in themselves.

Environmental awareness provides an excellent frame for appreciating our collective responsibilities. Charitable initiatives provided by the Sierra Club and The John Muir Trust have been very successful in advocating an active approach to environmental education. Their Award programmes encourage schools, families and youth groups to discover, enjoy and care for wild places found in their own neighbourhoods. Such a service brings benefits to all by turning us outwards, away from self-centred concerns, to a greater perspective and connects us with local community. Such programmes offer greater benefits than enhancing student learning – they also provide an active learning and purpose led approach which may support a wider range of teaching styles and strategies.

A pressing priority is to work closely in partnership with schools to develop skills and insight through facilitating and relating deep experiences back to everyday life. *A credible place then, is one which compliments and connects with other strategies within the social educational context.*

Rogues Lane

There is a lane that the children take each day they walk to school. Each morning they navigate the dog fouled streets. Sometimes they must dodge fly tipped rubbish and at other times evidence of salacious behaviours of the night. The local council claim they have no money to clean up and the school. There is a need for action.

Here is an opportunity afforded to the school if it could ask the right question, if it could frame its purpose more broadly. We should ask the question –at what point does responsibility for the education of our children stop? Is it at the school gate? No school exists apart from its locality. Even if the children are from another neighbourhood, the school is in the community itself. The schools on Rouges Lane can move to action – with both voice and participation, they could draw a communion through a shared concern -for it is everybody's street.

The story of Rogues Lane is not unique - there are many schools located in poor dysfunctional communities, vandalism, drugs, theft, knife crime are issues that cannot be ignored. Schools survive by buttoning down the hatches - but in doing so they lose an opportunity to engage and impact their communities.

Through the voice of children and the care for a community's context we can act and engage. This is compassion. More than just achieving learning targets, we can show children the power of participation and their voice. The best of our schools don't just work closely with their local communities but make the curriculum responsive to local needs too. Through the everyday work and relationships, a school may give to its community. In doing so, we find more meaningful learning, create socially responsible citizens and contribute to a better community.

ENGAGING WITH CHALLENGE

"I believe that work of excellence is transformational. Once a student sees that he or she is capable of excellence, that student is never quite the same"
Ron Berger

"... for education is possible only with children who look hopefully and joyfully upon the future" Alfred Adler

In 1915 the prominent educator, John Dewey, wrote a book entitled *Schools of Tomorrow* in which he complained that the conventional public school "is arranged to make things easy for the teacher who wishes quick and tangible results." Rather than fostering personal growth, he argued that "the ordinary school impressed the little one into a narrow area, into a melancholy silence, into a forced attitude of mind and body". This is as relevant today as it was 100 years ago.

Many students still have conceptions of learning bred by years of shallow, routine fact-pushing teaching, that prides itself on content directed from the front and by repeated prodding to perform to testing. Students, however, are not inert recipients and *build strategies* to deal with this daily grind of the knowledge dump. The conceptions of learning that they hold directly impacts upon their performance and development through these self-strategies (Hattie:1999). There are two major self-strategies that students develop and use when learning:

i) *Self-enhancement*: These are strategies that maintain the status-quo of self-image; to be seen as one wishes or believes one is; To do whatever it takes to preserve this concept of self by adopting strategies that maximise positive or minimise negative self-evaluations. Students self-enhance by biasedly selecting information which provides affirmation of their prior beliefs. Providing feedback to students is not enough - as the way individuals interpret your information is key to developing positive and valuable concepts of self.

ii) *Self-Verification:* These are testing strategies - seeking to test conceptions of self by adopting hypothesis-confirming strategies that allow for the best opportunities for self-expression. Those who use self-verification typically persist at the task after failure and tend to avoid tasks in which they have already reached an adequate level of performance. They make more optimistic predictions about their performance after initial failure and seek specifically unfavourable feedback so as to excel at their tasks (Hattie: 1999).

For students using Self-Verification strategies any initial success signifies a potential ability to be improved upon. On the other hand, Self-Enhancement strategies seek to avoid change and see challenge as personally threatening. A culture of achievement is developed when students seek feedback to verify rather than enhance efficacy and sense of self-worth.

There are three basic options open to a student as strategies to manage their relationship with performance and potentially challenging feedback:

1. Students can abandon the standards
2. Students can change the standard by setting lower goals in achievement at school
3. The Students can increase their effort

We can relate this relationship with learning to three different "Zones" in any cohort. The Impossibility Zone, The Purpose Zone and the Aspiration Zone.

1.The Impossibility Zone:

In the "Impossibility Zone" everything that we might assume is do-able and accessible is instead seen as a barrier by the student. With a shallow approach to learning and embedded self enhancement strategies they have made little or no progress – typically the child is not even at the starting point on their learning journey. They first need to have their attitudes and beliefs healed.   Yet the schools are under increasing pressure to get them to perform – to *"get on the bus"* and engage with learning. There is no space for a learning

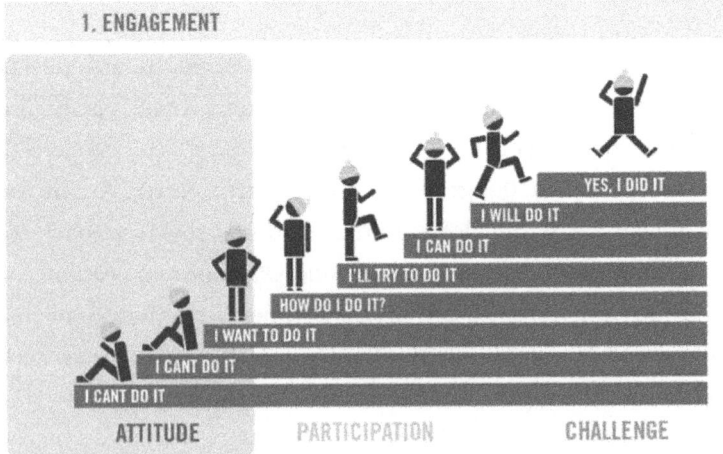

transaction. So it goes back to Alfred Adler's mention about the need for hope. According to Adler, the misbehaving child is a discouraged child. Whilst the skills sought are often related to numeracy and literacy, the skills actually needed are *facilitating skills*. The skills that will support the child to open up to re-engaging.

This might seem an obvious observation, however to understand the importance of recognising this we only need to look at how secondary schools in the United Kingdom used Pupil Premium funding in supporting the disengaged from disadvantaged backgrounds. Many schools put the funding into increased teaching time. As we have seen, and many are now beginning to realise, that just increasing the teaching time for students in the Impossibility Zone simply doesn't get the desired results. It is an expensive mistake for both child and school to assume that we can overlook what is going on in the child's greater social context. Re-engagement needs to be achieved by interventions that address what is going on with the deeper development needs of the individual child. Different individuals exposed to the same environment experience it, interpret it and react to it differently. [127] What leads a discouraged child onto further dysfunction and anti-social behaviour is their relationships and learnt characteristics. *What is learned can be unlearned and what has never been learned can be learned by way of new learning*. With the most difficult behaviours we can refer to research on *Criminogenic Needs* that show how improvements in key dynamic factors can make a significant impact on behaviour. Key factors are peer group associations, attitudes and values;

personal lack of thinking skills, self-control combined with lack of purpose or sense of responsibility. For those in the Impossibility Zone, school is a disempowering place and those with spirit will naturally resist being there. If we have not prepared the student for the performance demands required of them in the challenging subjects such as Mathematics, then it should not surprise us that they withhold effort and respect.[128] The traditional linear approach to progression, emphasis on performance and the priority on transmission of content over understanding only reaffirms a shallow and divisive relationship between pupil, teacher and learning. The talent myth is still commonly held with educators towards challenging subjects (and within families too) – where *you either can or can't do it*. The popular media doesn't help either. Jo Boaler's book "The Elephant in the Classroom" addresses this with regards to Mathematics.

To further make sense of a student's possible relationship with their study, we could contrast the needs of the student with the need of the school at each level of participation. To achieve this let's divide up the possible participation levels into just three possible zones. This allows for us to maintain a simple overview but still differentiates across the varying needs.

2.The Purpose Zone:
The next group of students predominantly the focus of leaderships attention. Students in The Purpose Zone represent the majority. Here it is the schools pressing priority to have

them take ownership of their studies. In the Purpose Zone students seek an answer to the question "what's the point?" They want to believe in something.

The common strategy for schools is to over-look the underlying need of the child and to address the school's business need. They provide hours of additional teaching support and demand more from teachers. Yet there is no space to accommodate the importance of meaning within the state school curriculum or the social contract between school, parent and student. In visiting many schools, one can begin to gauge the level of success quickly based on the quality of the community seen. You will see that the behaviours and level of respect shown around the school directly correlate with performance. The bulk of students get by according to what they must do. If the student body is without a sense of ownership in their learning, then one will feel the firm hand of top down control – a sense of muzzled participation. In a thriving learning community there exists many opportunities

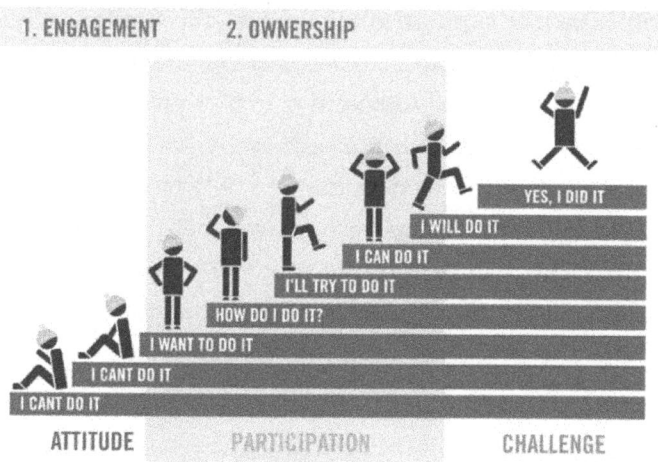

1. ENGAGEMENT   2. OWNERSHIP

YES, I DID IT
I WILL DO IT
I CAN DO IT
I'LL TRY TO DO IT
HOW DO I DO IT?
I WANT TO DO IT
I CANT DO IT
I CANT DO IT

ATTITUDE   PARTICIPATION   CHALLENGE

for participation, for student voices to be represented and for purpose to be drawn out. Students skilled with personal organisation and self-management skills will become more prone to self-directed learning and purpose. We could call this the Purpose Zone for that is both symptom and the prognosis.

For each child in the Purpose Zone the teacher sees a student who doesn't do the work in a way that is self-directed, but a child that looks for the easy short cut or answer. For the school it remains a real struggle for them to engage participation that shows ownership, pride and belonging. Skills and experiential opportunities are needed.

The student's need is to be purpose led. If they don't get that from family, then they seek it elsewhere. They need to have meaning – an answer to their question: "what's the point?" Even if you put the child into a different environment, you must still address their need for meaning and have it fit with the narrative that the school is trying to achieve.

As suggested, in bringing adventure in the classroom, there must be the structure available to provide the student with sufficient support to take ownership. Importantly, there too must be a purpose to the task in order to provide the student with the *fuel* to take this higher level of engagement. This fuel is called *intrinsic motivation*. Motivation is not something that can be determined solely by forces outside the individual, in-fact it has been shown that the use of extrinsic rewards can reduce intrinsic motivation levels.[129] Increasing intrinsic motivation involves affecting a student's thoughts, feelings and decisions.

Two common reasons given for not engaging are, "It's not worth it", and "I know I won't be able to do it".[130] *Intrinsic Motivation,* **M**, occurs when a student believes in the *Perceived Value*, **V**, of what is being learnt and also believes they have the *Personal Capacity*, **C**- an expectation that their effort is worthwhile:

$$M = VC$$

Students who are intrinsically motivated to learn at school seek out opportunities and challenges and go beyond requirements. The focus is on helping establish ways for students who are motivationally ready and able to achieve and, of course, to maintain and enhance their motivation.

3. The Aspiration Zone:

The last zone then could be referred to as the Aspiration or Challenge Zone. Care is needed however as aspiration is important to all children at all levels, regardless of their ability or their participation level. It is highlighted here as the students have more of the facilitating skills and are engaged with their learning yet may plateau. Schools have a need for those students that are coasting to seek further opportunities for growth- to go on to higher education or career routes as possibilities outside of what their social context or family might direct them to. There is a need for the child to take on new challenges, to push themselves. The mathematician, like the mountaineer does not stop just because they have reached one summit, they build on experiences towards bigger challenges, to the potential and excitement of new summits.

They too have a need for intervention, to overcome fixed mindsets or low aspirations for the future. Students can change the standard they work to by setting lower goals in achievement at school, accepting far below their capabilities as satisfactory. Similarly, with a purpose, students have cause to raise their own standards. As Thoreau said, "dreams are the touchstone of one's character" – we should add hopes too.

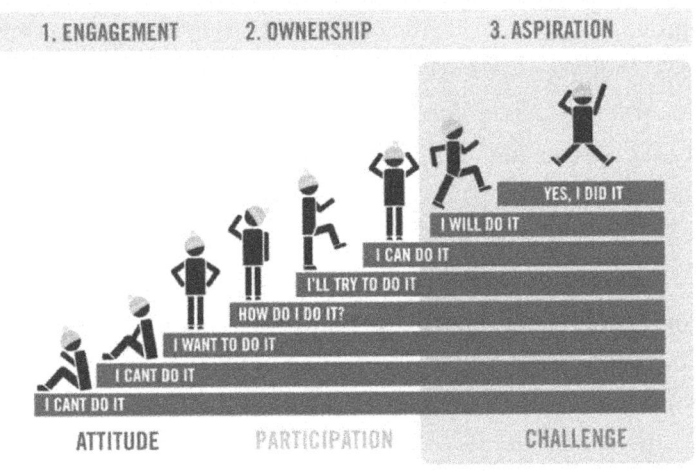

"Tell me what you expect me to know, and I may forget. Show me what you expect me to know, and I may remember. Involve me in what you expect me to know, and I will understand"
Chinese Proverb

OPTIMALLY ENGAGED

"Self-esteem from accomplishments, not compliments"
Ron Berger

In any group of people there will be a mix of characters. Typically, the participating student must put up with various types of disengaged colleagues, the disruptive character, the clown, and the disheartened. Just as we have referred to the misbehaving child being a discouraged child, we can see that there is a simple rationale for each of these behaviours.

In an explanation of behaviour, Dewey draws upon a distinction between experiences that are goal-relevant and experiences that are enjoyable. Dewey categorizes learning experiences into four quadrants: enjoyable and goal-relevant (termed *"optimally engaging");* neither enjoyable or goal relevant (termed "disinterest"); relevant but not enjoyable (termed "drudgery"); or enjoyable but not relevant (termed "fooling"). Dewey (1910/1991) suggests that the combination of enjoyment and goal relevance "defines *the ideal mental condition".*

A popular model that is influenced by Dewey's four quadrant model of Goal Relevance framework is known as *The Four P's Model.* Here the behaviours are categorised against the levels of Challenge (or stretch) and Support available. In this framework, the "optimally engaged" learner is the Participant. The other characters are the Prisoner, Protester and The Passenger. When we consider the perceived levels of challenge and support we not only have a way of classifying symptoms but a decision tool for diagnosis, prognosis and intervention.

In any group, there are those happy to coast along in their Comfort Zone, Dewey's fooling student who avoids challenge and enjoys high support levels. They are likely to accept the social norms– perhaps, even, they may seek to enforce them. They may outwardly be prosocial, but it is as a means rather than an end in itself. For now, they are happy to be a *Passenger*, whose propensity to engage is limited to self-interest. Without addressing their mindset, it may take a shock to wake them.

Figure - 16: *"The Four P's" Model of Participation*

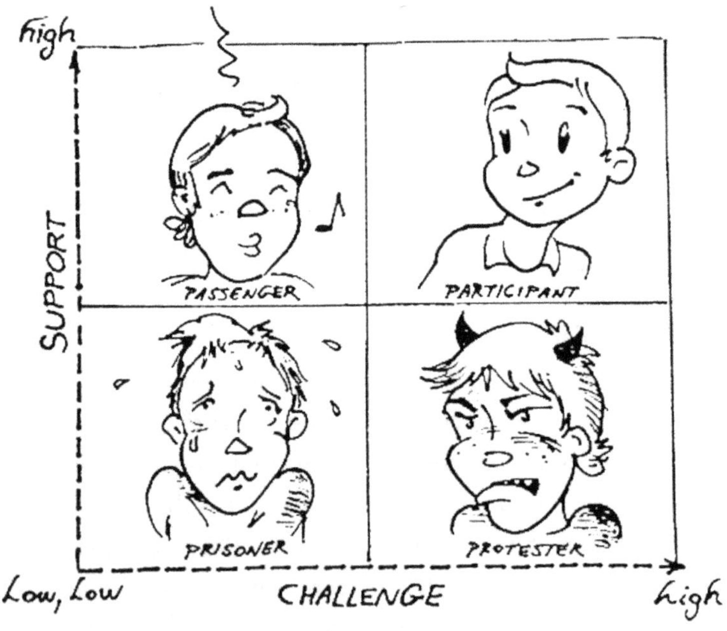

The *Prisoner* wants to be liberated. With a combination of progressive support and challenge we may free them from the thoughts and fears that keep them in their cell for one. Thus, the disinterested student who is closed to support or trying new things has the greatest amount to gain

The *Protestor* is someone we all will know. They are unhappy about their circumstances and want us to change it. They complain openly that they can' t and won't take part. They feel exposed, upset and defensive. Without support, they will feel stressed and attempt to escape their challenges or angrily plea for help. Any Prisoner can quickly become a protestor when pushed. A well performing student can transform into a difficult and surly class member if their support network disappears. Commonly seen when children endure their parents separation ... or at school, when relationships with teachers deteriorate or when school standards slip or classroom management is dysfunctional. The protestor is sadly more common that we would wish.

Lastly, we have the student who is optimally engaged. as an active *Participant*, has grown to look and discover for themselves. They happily engage with others with an open interest and sense of wonder that comes from Flow. It is here where a flourishing life is found.

The Four P's model is thus a useful tool for diagnosing the symptoms behind our classroom behaviours, however, perhaps more importantly, it also gives both prognosis and treatment. It provides us with an understanding of how best to help move all our students to performing at their best.

"One Move"

On nearly every mountain you will find a tricky bit. You will find it near the summit after the point when you have invested everything and have only two choices... to go on or turn back. Mountaineers call it the Bad Step On leading an expedition to Mt Meru in the Everest region of Nepal, a client of mine recently had their encounter. Overwhelmed with self-doubt at an unexpected task beyond their experience- the bad step effect kicked in – to withdraw effort and retreat.

"I can't do it" they said.

In feeling overwhelmed it is difficult to generate sufficient commitment from within. Sometimes unlocking the bad step we have to look to someone else. They have the key.

"So let's look at what's required here?" I said, breaking it down into simple steps and pausing for a moment provided time to open up doors.

"Do you really think I can do it?"

Their statement was really a question – "Yes I think you can do it". And he started to climb.... many people do. I knew he was going to make it. One move, they found the commitment to act.

We can find ourselves in situations like that, it doesn't have to be on a Himalayan peak. We might come across such scenarios in life's tasks – be it opportunities or challenges, relationships or responsibilities. Sometimes the climber has the key themselves and just doesn't know it yet ...." you can finish this if you really want to".

The inner cheerleader says...but sometimes we just need to hear it from another person we trust. In pulling together, we will ultimately find the commitment to take on that move.

Here's the question I sometimes find myself contemplating: - Have I climbed a mountain of 16,000 feet or did I just make one significant move?

Life can be that simple.

Thanks to Jamie Holding IFMGA for sharing this story.

EMPOWER WITH PURPOSE

"It is their adventure and if they tell you about it, it is because
they hope that you will understand"
(Charlton :1980)

Adventure is a kind of story - a way of construing certain experiences. It depends on how we each see the situation and what meaning it has to us.[131] There are times when the experience itself matters far more than any learning or performance improvement that might immediately arise from it. Dewey writes of experiences carrying people into the future, He describes an educative experience as one that: *"... arouses curiosity, strengthens initiative, and sets up desires and purposes that are sufficiently intense to carry a person over dead places in the future."* (Dewey 1938, 31) As meaning makers we see the world as it matters to us. A purpose transforms the personal relevance of learning. Consider *The emotional processing involved with reliving an experience of elevation or awe. – this* may turn out to be of greater lasting value than the purely cognitive processing. Fulsome, purposeful experiences simultaneously satisfy several developmental needs. With them we begin deeper, more adventurous learning journeys.

It's important that young people think about what they enjoy doing, what they really care about. In his book Dr Peter Benson called these "sparks," and just about all young people can identify their sparks.[132] The next thing you must help them identify is what they value—what bothers or upsets them about the world today, what they really like, what they could see improving upon—and then bringing that together by asking them, "How can you use your personal skills or strengths for addressing these problems?" We really have to listen to young people and help them to start talking about purpose and meaning, giving them a chance to really talk and reflect.

As a parent or educator you can help your own children discover a sense of purpose by simply asking about what's most important to them and talking about one's own sense of purpose in life. To help someone begin a path to their life purpose may be the greatest service you could give. Kendall Bronk is a researcher at Claremont Graduate University who studies how purpose impacts wellbeing throughout life. Her studies show that young people are hungry for purpose—and without it, they tend to be uninterested in school and more prone to psychological issues down the road. Contrarily, those with purpose look forward to greater wellbeing.

Bronk defines purpose as having a goal in life that you care deeply about and that contributes to the world beyond yourself in some productive sense. In some cases, she has found that all it takes to get young people started down a path of purpose is to engage them in deep, probing conversations, which prompt them to reflect on their interests and values. Fortunately, she also found that purpose is pretty malleable. It's reasonably easy to help young people think about purpose and identify and even start working toward that purpose. Just having children talk about the things that matter in their lives significantly increased their reporting of purpose. However, it can be short lived - If you can induce a sense of purpose that quickly, you can also lose it if it's not continually used.

Professor Albert Bandura's Social Learning Theory was an important contribution.[133] He proposed that difference in self-efficacy correlates to fundamentally different world views. People with high self-efficacy generally believe that they are in control of their own lives, that their own actions and decisions shape their lives, while people with low self-efficacy may see their lives as outside their control. Such evidence speaks directly to the outcomes of transformative learning, in that the assumptions, beliefs and values of individuals (as a result of their level of self-efficacy), can potentially shape the direction of the critical discourse taking place in the classroom, based on their feelings of either being in control or not in control of their destiny. [134] Such considerations will obviously influence the relationship between a student and teacher and learning environment.[135]

Share your own purpose in life. By hearing from a parent, "Here is what gives my life purpose or meaning," makes it easier for a young person to relate to, and more amenable and impactful.

Having young people focus on the things for which they're *grateful* can be a springboard for figuring out how they want to give back; about ways in which they can give back and help others.

You have to start small. Let's say your children really care about ending homelessness, despite the overwhelming complexity it is helpful to show that even the smallest of steps matter. What are the ways you can start with? In the end, one might only have to begin to share their appreciation of another's plight. Connecting young people to opportunities to act on their personally meaningful goals is critical. Young people sometimes identify big lofty goals, and if you can help them think of ways they can immediately get involved, it's really impactful.

Research by Bronk and colleagues found that anyone who'd identified a purpose in life—felt they had a direction and they were working toward achieving it. Their age didn't matter; They reported having very high levels of wellbeing. Perhaps this is unsurprising. After all Aristotle spoke of this connection. Wellbeing to him *(or eudaemonia)* required virtue which he called *"arete"* and a level of rationality. Arete is the goodness from the pursuit of excellence. It refers to those aspects of wellbeing that transcend immediate self-gratification and connect people to something larger. Consider the Olympic champion, Usain Bolt: the training it takes to be a great athlete is not pleasurable but fulfilling one's purpose as a great runner brings happiness. [136] This sense of connection drives the pursuit of excellence and wellbeing.

Reflections from visiting an
Expeditionary Learning Classroom
By Jon Clarke, Walsall Academy

"What strikes me is the students ability during the Crew group session in the morning to focus themselves. [137] They are active in supporting each other and have an open discussion on a theme. As they head towards their final days at WHEELS[138] they will craft a final expedition with some social service element which will then go on public display as their passage. The Crew I was with were in their last year and preparing for the final stages of education worried about results, college places, getting the grades to go to a good college and all of the other issues associated with being 17 or 18. The Crew leader started every day with some music on a theme to get the groups ready, then a quote which would be discussed and shared and then some formal discussion of activity all straight from the how to be a good EL teacher folder. He had been doing this for a number of years so knew his Crew well and was able to support but also challenge them. The oracy and the ability of the students to express their thoughts and learning journeys was amazing. It always strikes me how confident and accepting these students are of each other and of each other's thoughts. It never feels like tokenism as it would in a citizenship session in a UK school.

What you see when you are in a room? The desks are horse shoe shaped and the tops of are white boards, so the students can be more interactive in their lessons. In English I had thought the students learning would come from their text book. But I was wrong, they were also investigating slavery, globalisation and ethical issues. So here they talk about debriefs and takeaways. The young people at

WHEELS are good at understanding what has gone on in the past and looking towards the future.

The next surprise was their concept of student led parent conferences. Throw away the notion of the parents evening it is not like that. The students work towards self-assessment in every lesson so that they are fully aware of the level at which they are working. They complete reflective self-evaluation forms which then set targets on how to improve. These form the basis of the parent, student and crew leader discussion. So, the student has to be aware of their own levels and the next steps which they then need to take. I can say from seeing it that the students take it very seriously and will try and negotiate better grades if they can. I believe that linked into this is the conduct of the students. I did not see teachers shouting or even having crossed words with students. Conversations were common place much as I am used to where we try to find out the reason for a student's conduct then sort the issue not just shout. When I asked the teachers, they believe that the NYC EL schools do have very good conduct due to the ethos and the crew time and the service component of their school lives. In my own school the social responsibility and conduct are linked to what we do in personal tutorial time which is similar, but we could, as they do here, do much more. I believe that the introduction of the student led conference at my school will place far more of the ownership of learning into the hands of the students making them more accountable and leaders of their own learning."

A Good Listener- The Story of a School
By Gwyn ap Harri, XP School

What do you remember from school? I bet it was something you created that you were proud of, or an experience out of the normal classroom environment, or a relationship you established. I bet it invokes a powerful emotional response - good or bad. I bet it makes a good story. I have asked many people this question and not once did I hear a reply along the lines of, "Well, I had to fill in a lot of worksheets, but I remember this one worksheet - it changed my life forever!"

At XP, we carry the idea of narrative throughout our curriculum planning. In fact, this is where we start - we construct the story of the learning expedition. This narrative is the backbone to our purpose, we hang our knowledge and skills off it. At the end, we create something, and we reflect on how this journey has helped us progress academically and our character grow.

The notion of 'narrative' in the learning process is a powerful one. Awe in Action gives me many ways to reflect on our student narratives and therefore improve them by making them more memorable, authentic and purposeful.

In the end, aren't we all just a bunch of stories? Here's one of my own stories... In February 2012, I found myself bewildered in San Diego, USA. What was supposed to be a jovial trip out with some school colleagues - my first visit to America - with the vague idea to look at something called 'project-based learning', ended up with me making the most important professional decision of my life. I wandered around the school I was visiting, High Tech High, for three days, with no real questions I could deliver, only a quivering "thank you" to the CEO, Larry Rosenstock. At some point during the last evening, after a few fish tacos and a few more drinks, I announced to my colleagues that because of what I'd seen, there was nothing for it but to start my own school. The next year, I found myself in

Amherst, Massachusetts at the headquarters of Expeditionary Learning with Ron Berger and Scott Hartl. Just before we left, Scott leaned in and said, "you know this all started with you guys? Gordonstoun, Outward Bound, Kurt Hahn..." I looked over at my friend and colleague, Andy Sprakes, who seemed to know what he was on about, as I didn't have a clue. On the flight back, Andy explained that Kurt Hahn created Gordonstoun school and Outward Bound - that Outward Bound USA came from the UK originally, and that EL came from that. Neither of us knew that the Aberdovey OB centre was where it had all started, but in April 2014, we were told by Dr Anna Switzer, an American EL school designer who was with us to induct our new school staff, the whole OB history while we participated in our first staff outdoor expedition in Aberdovey itself. She could even point out the exact house where Lawrence Holt and Kurt Hahn cooked up the idea.

Since then we have grown XP Schools and despite our different approach to most other schools and our catchment, we have been rated Outstanding in all categories by the state Inspectorate. Looking back now, some people might call it fate. I prefer serendipity myself. Either way, it just goes to show that you've got to get out there to come back.

-o0o-

Gwyn ap Harri is the CEO of XP School Trust, a mainstream multi-academy trust based in Doncaster, UK, which is heavily inspired by High Tech High and Expeditionary Learning, USA, and therefore The Outward Bound Trust which started in Aberdovey, Wales.

The first day of secondary school, their students get on a bus in Doncaster and travel to Aberdovey for a four day Outward Bound experience. Here they explore the guiding question, 'What is Crew?' and during every activity they reflect on the character traits of courage, respect, craftsmanship and quality, compassion and integrity. When they get back to school, they do exactly the same in their classrooms.

DELIVERING HIGH IMPACT LEARNNG

"The quality of an education system cannot exceed
the quality of its teachers"[139]

In addressing the whole child, we need to embrace the broadest range of approaches to learning. For too long the pedagogy of learning has been put into a binary between schools of thought - the Constructive verses the Social; Rigour verses Breadth; Academic performance verses Employability skills ... and so on. The traditionalists will argue with the progressives as if their approaches were entirely exclusive – in fact blinded to the continuum of learning that together they afford. Each has their place.

Understanding and skill development require a more active means for unlocking the latent potential in each learner. The argument for the transmission of learning content overlooks the necessity of applying the best means for result. Facts and memorisation may matter, just as discovery and experiential matter, yet each asks for an entirely different approach for best effect. One approach is measurable and cheap- the other messy and involved.

In choosing the appropriate method of delivery we must make full use of the teacher's skills and compliment the material with the mind. Like song, reason is not set as one tone and the result is equally lacking if the performer cannot access the rich scale of variation.

Thus, there are three fundamental challenges for the traditional approach to recognise and address:

1) *Role of emotions in focusing attention: Prosocial emotions can act as a strong motivator in education, for it provides students with a purpose beyond themselves and the classroom*

2) *Importance of first hand experiences*

3) *Building in personal meaning from a student's point of view.*

Just as E.D. Hirsch argues for an essential base of knowledge for 'Cultural Literacy', *should we not use the same argument to ensure an equivalent reservoir of healthy experiences and socio-emotional skill exists for the student to draw upon?* Educators need to be equipped with training before their lessons can move away from "Teacher directed" unadventurous learning. To be able to unlock their student's potential, they first must be able to impart the attitudes and skills for supporting self-directed and collaborative learning. Active learning is part of this shift towards becoming educationally wise. It can be defined as anything that "involves students in doing things and thinking about what they are doing" [140] But it is not busyness for busyness sake! The appropriate use of active learning requires planning but rewards with richer opportunities "to talk and listen, read, write, and reflect as student's approach course content" [141] This develops not only students' knowledge but also their skills, personal abilities and a care to use them.

ELEVATED FOR ACTION

I slept and dreamt that life was joy. I awoke and saw that life was service.
I acted and behold service was joy.
Rabindranath Tagore

Now, more than any other anytime in our lives, has there been such a need for a concerted and deliberate effort in addressing values within education[142]. From our actions we can have an influence much greater than we can know. Our excellence is a conduit for others to grow; it may have an unfathomable potential to the individual. Unwittingly it adds to humanity.

It's important to note that your efforts to induce awe in students will fall on some deaf ears. For example, Dr Keltner found that not everyone is prone to awe - particularly those who are not comfortable changing their outlook on the world but that shouldn't keep teachers from trying to induce prosocial emotions in students. Psychologist Paul Piff speculates, *"There's good reason to think that students who don't experience awe could benefit from those who do. For example, through the contagious effects of positive emotion, increased solidarity and cooperation, social facilitation, and benefiting from others' egalitarianism."*

You will no doubt see clear differences between the awe experienced in the natural world and the moral elevation created by witnessing excellence in others and I may be criticised for seeming to have the two "superimposed" for my argument, however ultimately the message in this book is to use these experiences – it is a call to action. Responding to the inspiring excellence of others can indeed create awe but it is likely to need excellent facilitation as well to turn that emotion into action – it can be a catalyst for caring, but, without attention being given to *"now what?"* (i.e. how we follow up and use them), the power and usefulness of the experience may be forgotten. Our experiences of awe and elevation, admiration and gratitude should be harnessed into prosocial action.

As educators we must be determined that positive prosocial behaviours and common values of humanity prevail. We must embrace the power of social action and community in our practice. Many of our students are still being trained to perform to test under the politicised guise of neo-traditionalism. We watch as children in these environments withdraw from criticism and slowly become spectators in their own lives. The social contract between state school and child remains one-way with an emphasis on Return-On-Investment rather than personal growth. It's no small wonder then why children become adept in developing strategies for avoiding the risk of failure, become removed from prosocial participation and are susceptible more to a providence of fate than to their industry and courage. How do we get young people to see themselves for what they really are in the wider context?

Active learning approaches, if planned well, are a very good start. Of the many approaches, Expeditionary Learning stands out. The protocols and strategies of Expeditionary Learning (as developed and freely shared by EL Education) achieve more than academic achievement. The collaborative approach of Crew holds peers accountable. It goes beyond the acquisition of problem solving and oracy skills to address qualities of character. The EL student develops an ethic of excellence and feels the capacity inherent in themselves and others for goodness. Through their work towards mastery, students gain an appreciation of beauty. Through their action[143] they tap into purpose, values and civic responsibilities. Here lies great potential for experiencing a humanity in action. It is essential and has important real-world implications. Here lies the heart that is missing from the Traditional Approach to the education of our children.

Those who work tirelessly within our education system know only too well the waste that results from not tackling disengagement, disillusionment and inertia in learning. It is testament that in a time of unprecedented wealth and technological development, the school life for many children (and teachers) remains, enforced and disempowering. Too many policy makers still view education as a process of "filling minds" rather than growing sustainable adults. There is no space for considerations of civic and moral praxis, lost opportunities for the development of a practical wisdom that leads to a more stable and flourishing lives.

Education when seen as a matter of processing and grading - sorting through and children like any other raw resource has come to a juncture. At the time of writing, too many good teachers are leaving the profession, retention is poor, recruitment requires considerable incentive– these actions belie a conflict in the profession's very purpose and worth to society. So perhaps we leave with too many unanswered questions- what is the purpose of education to you? Where does your responsibility end? Are you driven by the values that matter?

Some policy makers and outspoken critics of schools assert that "it is naïve to think schools can do much to ameliorate the effects of inequality". Even asserting that as "the impact of the environment on children's attainment... is fairly negligible...so schools don't matter much."[144] Whilst outspoken criticism, arrogant and naïve views make for headlines and sell newspapers, they also give air to extreme policy advocates for discrimination and in instances even social engineering. Today, in the twenty first century, erroneous inferences are still being drawn from interpretations of "heritability" and are being generalised to entire social groups to emphasise a supposed non-malleability of socio-economic inequality and intelligence. There is a polarisation and a growing popularity of apologist views that proclaim the failure of meritocracy and the irrelevance of social capital and environment to support social mobility. The world view of a small genetic superior elite should be alarming to any student of history. Such views are a toxic distortion and misrepresentation of liberal values. Meritocracy, personal freedom, personal potential and opportunity are clearly of value to any free society. The biological sciences have clearly moved beyond Galton and the binary of genes versus environment - nature versus nurture – to appreciate and start to understand how genes and environments interact in multiple and complex ways.[145] In education, environmental pressures, as stress from welfare, health, income uncertainty, and social capital - the poverty of opportunity almost always matter for a child's learning.

We must address the erroneous linear basis of classical economic market thinking as applied to human capital- our children's education and futures. No discourse stands alone. An appreciation for the opportunities and progress that arise from connectivity in ideas, and people, comes when we understand the importance of Complexity and the power of Culture in driving human behaviour.

With such a back drop, the health-giving experiences and potential for supporting the skills of executive function (such as attention, appreciation and autonomy) as a foundation is clear. The chronic stress of poverty has need for providing for inoculative situations that play a part in protecting children through useful experiences of resilience, determination and perseverance. The school curriculum needs to begin engaging with the affective nature of children more positively. Negative emotional appraisals and responses are as important to address as are poor grades- indeed the two are in most cases completely interrelated.

Developing the vital skills of our children is far more than merely raising their perceived level of confidence. In providing young people with wonderful and awe-inspiring experiences from which they can build skills and attitudes we give them the seeds to grow prosocial and altruistic values. Connecting them with something bigger than themselves we turn our children outwards. We all benefit greatly from more contact with wilderness and nature – the combination of physical engagement and immersion in the wild, fuels our emotional and physical wellbeing. Nature's role for our children's health and wellbeing should not be underestimated.

Small changes can have a big impact. Many school leaders unwittingly remove one of their best opportunities for positive change when they act to cut back Core Experiences, such as Outdoor Adventurous Learning, from their strategy. Rather than becoming more connected in their approach they lower the horizon for opportunity and curtail relationships in their learning community.

The Outward Bound Trust effectively connects young people to nature, to themselves and to each other. Through real challenge and through adventurous expeditionary journeys comes the experience of compassion, resilience, respect, courage and the will to better oneself. However, adventurous learning experiences are not univariate, linear or independent – authentic and impactful experiences respect the complexity of our student's social emotional development.

Delivering impactful Outdoor Adventurous Learning requires a respect for student context and a commitment to relationships that can only be supported by close partnerships. Peak experiences have the potential to be *turning points* when meaningful. If our children can return to them over and over and link them into a personal progression, then through these experiences we have added to their positive *trajectory*. Your school has this possibility if only the value of core experiences and importance of collaborative partnerships can be seen.

Developing the skill and attitudes for attention, ability, appreciation and authorship may help as stepping stones. As habits, they may host new behaviours, the seeds of virtue. Through action (or inaction) a given situation may be the turning point needed. If recognised and nurtured, this could be the first possible iteration of a trophic cascade - a potential trajectory unfolding throughout one's life and relationships. Through better connected work and purpose, a small change has a big impact.

We here bring our attention to the heart of the matter – delivering high impact learning. *"Who we are, or who we might become is inseparable from who we are with, where we are, and what we are doing.* In developing character and skills for life we must carefully consider the context of students and understand their relationships with self, others and their learning. In considering the concept of Expeditionary Learning we pay respect to the situated nature of human activity and the importance of continuity of relationships. Ongoing positive relationships and a culture of practice are important features of the enlightened school.

Through meaningful work the student has cause to increase their authorship. Their learning must be connected to a purpose. If that work is original and is connected in action with their community, it lasts for life. *Sustainable change requires much more than one trip or a few weeks out of their life. Students need to see their lives as part of the solution by what they advocate, what they purchase, and in their voice. To see that they can create change, will alter the way they act throughout life and in all of life, they become responsible, part of the solution.*

All students deserve an education based on joy and passion in learning - the chance to become exceptional scholar's, successful in employment and ethical citizens. The potential for the Expeditionary Learning approach within schools stands out. We can share the vision of hope from inspirational educator's such as Ron Berger or Larry Rosenstock.[146] For this to be so, there is some distance to travel for us all. We must break the mandate of delivering content for its own sake. There must be reason to do the work well, not just because someone wants it that way. Central to any learning community must be humanity and opportunity. An opportunity to learn collaboratively and build knowledge through intellectual interaction in an environment that addresses the students' personal needs.

Let us aspire for more positive social experiences to support qualities of behaviour in children. Let us work to build learning cultures around trust and beautiful student work. With compassion, care and love let us connect with the skills and courage needed for a more peaceful and just world. Something that will make us all proud.

EPILOGUE

The below quote from poet Gary Snyder makes me think of how the teacher on the front line holds their passion for learning. Day after day they deal with difficult behaviours, pressures with assessment targets, increased workloads, policy changes, uncertainty, turnover in staff and leadership ... those who still love teaching, who still see with young eyes and care deeply for the child - who plan and aspire for their pupils beyond the classroom, are role models for our time, diamonds of humanity, lights of wisdom, our ambassadors of compassion. What source do they tap into that radiates such energy? This is the stuff of awe and admiration; in action they elevate us all.

In my work I have the privilege to meet some of these people - they are the ones challenging the status quo, leading and working overtime to get their children opportunities such as going on an Outward Bound course. Let's recognise and cherish them.

"Range after range of mountains.
Year after year after year.
I am still in love."

Gary Snyder

ACKNOWLEDGEMENTS

This is the product of many good people and occasions. I am grateful for the inspiration, permission and/or contribution from the following people: Nick Barrett, Kim Parry LVO, William Ripley MVO, Galeo Saintz, Gwyn Ap Harri, Jon Spears, Hollie Jones, Andy Thorpe, Jo Fromant, Jamie Holding, Janek Mamino, Claire Waring, Christian Kirasic, Gus Tyk, Sean Comiskey, Dr Dacher Keltner, Dr Randall Williams, Dr Tom Harrison, Bonnie Whitecloud, Manataka American Indian Council, Simon Waring, Mary and Michael Long, Rob Smith, Sally Ryder-Taylor, Dave Challis, Max Giradeau and to Jon Clarke for his unwavering loyalty and drive for our mission.

Special thanks to Ron Berger for his inspiration and example which has moved me to write. I most am grateful to him and to EL Education for letting me share their important work. I am indebted to the Directors of The Outward Bound Trust for placing their trust in this work.

I am blessed with the love of my family, especially my ever-patient wife Sarah and wonderful son James. I owe a life time of gratitude to my parents and grandparents who have been the foundation for my growth and an anchor for my hopes. Mary, Peter, Margret, Bill, Eileen, Anne & Helena, thank you for your endless support.

I take all responsibility for any omission or error. My intentions are good.
KPL

NOTES

PREFACE

[1] *Stephen raised the profile of Teen cancer and funding between chemotherapy sessions, raising £5 million before he passed away. Logan's Torch, a 6-year-old raised £36000 for dogs for the deaf. Ryan Raised $800.000 for Water Aid. Emma has courageously stood up to National Rifle Association, gun lobbyists and politicians. She is a student at Marjory Stoneman Douglas High School, speaking in the days after 17 people were left dead after a preventable mass shooting.*

INTRODUCTION

[1] *Hahn 1965 p3. Harrogate Address Outward Bound*
[2] *This work looks only at the positive encounters of the sublime such as elicited by aesthetic beauty and moral excellence. We are interested in positive awe experiences that lead to greater momentary well-being parasympathetic arousal, and prosocial feelings. Awe, however has its dark side; it is also elicited by threat-based experiences mediated by increased feelings of powerlessness and fear. Gordon, A., Stellar, J. et al (2017)*
[3] *Great deeds that inspire us are typically uncommon, but we can achieve many small things with great love!*
[4] *With the emphasis on Outdoor Adventurous Education*
[5] *Tom Lilley (1998)*
[6] *Richard Schusterman (2006) Thinking Through the Body, Educating for the Humanities: A Plea for Somaesthetics*

PART ONE FINDING AWE IN ACTION

[1] *We might think we are sharing the same experience, yet, in Awe, each of us are on our own. It's no surprise then that emotions of moral elevation, such*

as *Awe, are regarded to have powerful implications for quality of life. Each individual is uniquely their own.*

[2] *Many emotional responses greatly move us, sometimes the frame is from a loss, a regret, or shame in others it is a revelation, accolade or gift. We are only interested in the later. In its broadest sense awe can assume many forms and not every instance is useful for our study and the context matters. There is no elevation or virtue in response to incidents of sheer terror and yet if we are in safety, a tiger may evoke our admiration.*

[3] *Wilson, M, (2002)*

[4] *Dacher is also the author of Born to Be Good: The Science of a Meaningful Life, The Power Paradox and a co-editor of The Compassionate Instinct: The Science of Human Goodness.*

[5] *Refers to an Article by Will Storr, "A Better Kind of Happiness" – New Yorker, July (2016)*

[6] *Chang, S.-M. (2016, July). From her paper on Meaning-Cantered Positive Education. development and implementation of life education in Taiwan: A meaning-cantered positive education. Invited paper presented at the 9th Biennial International Meaning Conference in Toronto, ON.*

[7] *Keltner, D. Haidt, J. (2003)*

[8] *John, O.P. & Srivastava, S (1999) The Big Five trait taxonomy: history, measurement, and theoretical perspectives. In Pervin & John, (Eds.) Handbook of personality: Theory and research (pp 102-138)*

[9] *Rudd, M., Vohs, K. and Aaker , J. (2012), Awe Expands People's Perception of Time, Alters Decision Making, and Enhances Well-Being*

[10] *Keltner and Haidt (2003)*

[11] *Kyle Smith, N & Cacioppo, John & Larsen, Jeff & L Chartrand, Tanya. (2003). May I have your attention, please: Electrocortical responses to positive and negative stimuli. Neuropsychologia. 41. 171-83.*

[12] *It is well-documented (Baumeister, Bratslavsky, Finkenauer, & Vohs:2001).*

[13] *Piff , Dietze, Feinberg, Keltner (2015) Awe, the Small Self, and Prosocial Behaviour*

[14] *Arguably, seeing someone perform a virtuous act can be interpreted as a signal of trustworthiness, which could explain the link between witnessing such acts and the physiological sensations associated with moral elevation. Algoe and Haidt (2009) (Zak, Kurzban, & Matzner, (2005).*

[15] *(Haidt, 2000, 2003)*

[16] *(Haidt, 2000, 2003; Keltner & Haidt, 2003).*

[17] *Silvers and Haidt (2008) suggest that some of these sensations might be caused by the release of the hormone oxytocin, which rises in levels when people receive signals of trust.*

[18] *(Ekman, 1992; Scherer, 1984)*

[19] *(Haidt, 2000, 2003).*

[20] *(e.g., Kant, 1959; Singer, 1981) and psychologists (e.g., Eisenberg, 2000; Gilligan, 1982; Kohlberg, 1969)*

[21] *Schnall, Simone; Jean Roper; Daniel Fessler (2010)*

[22] *from Rosseau "Emile; or, Treatise on Education", 1762,*

[23] *Haidt (2003).*

[24] *Batson, O'Quinn, Fulty, Vanderplass, & Isen, (1983); Batson & Shaw, 1991; Eisenberg, Fabes, Miller, Fultz, Shell, Mathy, et al., 1989; Hoffman, 1982).*

[25] *Haidt (2007). The new synthesis in moral psychology. Science 316.5827: 998–1002. Influential article by Jonathon Haidt that proclaims a "new synthesis" in moral psychology, drawing on evolutionary, social, and cognitive psychology, and neuroscience.*

[26] *In 1968 millions of people, mostly children, were starving due to a military blockade of Biafra, the former Eastern Region of Nigeria. The United Nations and most national governments, expressed a reluctance to become involved in what was officially considered an internal Nigerian affair. Secretary General of the United Nations, U Thant, refused to support an airlift. The ruling Labour Party of the United Kingdom, which together with*

the USSR was supplying arms to the Nigerian military. A small band of civilian pilots decided to act. Impelled by the suffering that they saw they stepped up and went out to help. They came from around world, they left their commercial flights to volunteer to fly rickety old planes such as DC-3s illegally into the hostile region. Some died doing so. The only landing strip was a road clearing in the forest - called Uli. The flights were undertaken under cover of darkness and without lights to avoid attacking Nigerian aircraft who maintained air superiority during the day, supported by Soviet fishing trawlers offshore monitoring the flights. Each aircraft made as many as four round-trips each night into Uli. Aid reaching the dying children was devoid of official backing, the task of keeping the children alive while the fighting raged was taken up by the churches. This airlift was the first major civilian airlift in history, and the largest of any civilian relief effort of any kind since.

Bernard Kouchner and a group of French volunteer doctors working in Biafra concluded that a new aid organization that would prioritize the welfare of victims irrespective of national or religious boundaries was needed, went on to found Médecins Sans Frontières or Doctors Without Borders in 1971

https://www.irishtimes.com/news/ghosts-of-biafra-1.73370

[27] The research of John Gottman and Robert Levenson (1992) on marriage and interpersonal relationships showed the number of positive interactions outweighs negative interactions in successful relationships and by a ratio of five to one. (Gottman: 1994)

[28] In his later year, Leo Tolstoy published a parable about forgiveness called "Wisdom of Children". 1885. Each dialogue has a title based on a social or moral issue- the irony in each shows the wisdom of the child's questioning being ignored of adults' thoughtless words and deeds.

.http://www.nonresistance.org/docs_pdf/Tolstoy/Wisdom_of_Children.pdf

[29] Hannah Arendt, Vita Activa and the Human Condition (Chapter 1) of The Human Condition. Chicago: University of Chicago Press, 1958.

[30] *Inspired by reading http://deepecologyphoto.blogspot.co.uk/*

[31] *Johnson-Laird and Oatley*

[32] *Emotions can occur through automatic appraisal, with little awareness, and involuntary response changes in expression and psychology. (Eikman)*

[33] *Ortony,(1988)*

[34] *Baerveldt and Verheggen suggest that the social patterning of experience is to be understood through enactivism, pp401. Embodiment, Enaction, and Culture: By Christoph Durt, Thomas Fuchs, Christian Tewes*

[35] *The influential psychologist Jerome Bruner, introduced enaction as 'learning by doing'*

[36] *Randall Williams (2011) "The Impact of Residential Adventure Education on Primary School Pupils": Development is in the domain of the observer: all that matters is to maintain one's internal consistency – self -integrity- in changing external contexts. This explains why the process of personal development is so difficult to measure. Nowak et al (2000) apply the concept of emergence to self-belief, showing that it reconciles the fact that the self consists of many diverse cognitive and affective elements with the more global way of looking at the self, embodied in notions such as self-esteem" See also a report published on the RSA's webpage. The Benefits of Outdoor Adventure, Feb, 2011 The www.RSA.org.*

[37] *The consideration of complexity stands in stark contrast to those policy influencers who hold on to a linear, deterministic view and this is clearly most acute when it comes to addressing the investment needs of education and social mobility.*

[38] *Mihaly Csikszentmihalyi coined the term "flow" in his seminal book, Beyond Boredom and Anxiety: Experiencing Flow in Work and Play (1975).*

[39] *See Williams R. (2012) -supports these points respectivley by referencing: Nelson (2004). Building blocks and learning. Complicity: An International Journal of Complexity and Education, Cilliers,(1998) Complexity and postmodernism, and Nowak (2004). Dynamic minimalism: Why less is more in psychology. Personality and Social Psychology Review.*

[40] Manuel Velasquez, Claire Andre, Thomas Shanks, S.J., and Michael J. Meyer (1988). "Ethics and Virtue" in Ethics V1 N3. Spring

[41] Bem, (1972); Olson & Stone, (2005) As referenced in Principals of Social Psychology, Ebook ISBN:978-1-946135-20-9 5.3 Changing Attitudes by Changing Behaviour

[42] From Mick Waters on Centralisation, OFSTED and Brilliant Schools – p.112, Posted on 18th April 2016 https://pivotaleducation.com/mick-waters-centralisation-ofsted-brilliant-schools-pp112/

[43] Brendtro, Brokenleg et. al. (1990). Reclaiming Youth at Risk: Our Hope for the Future. Bloomington,

PART TWO: SKILLS FOR LIFE

[44] K. Anders Ericsson, Ralf Th. Krampe, and Clemens Tesch-Romer (1993) The Role of Deliberate Practice in the Acquisition of Expert Performance. Psychological Review. 1993, Vol. 100. No. 3, 363-406

[45] But then recommends changing the structure. In his persuasive book, "Education Is Upside-Down: Reframing Reform to Focus on the Right Problem" Kalenze argues that instead of education fitting students for the world that they are to inhabit it attempts to fit the world to our students. They need to be exposed to the pressures of performance. That character will come through high stakes examination and by ensuring student apply themselves to work Kalenze uses the metaphor of a funnel. He claims that the funnel of education is upside down, and there is too much waste.

[46] Championed as brightest student in the UK and as quiz show winner, Christodoulou wrote a controversial book. The Seven Myths, criticising some long-held tenants of education. She argues that learning through discovery learning is criminally wasteful. "It's very difficult to learn from the real world. Apples dropped from trees for centuries, but only Newton discovered the laws of gravity. As he said, we have to stand on the shoulders of giants."

Memory of knowledge will "cause" skilled performance. The seven myths, according to Daisy Christodoulou

- Facts prevent understanding
- Teacher-led instruction is passive
- The 21st century fundamentally changes everything
- You can always just look it up
- We should teach transferable skills
- Projects and activities are the best way to learn
- Teaching knowledge is indoctrination

[47] Christopher Peterson and Martin Seligman and colleagues

[48]From this they created a systematic classification in which the six virtues are made up of 24-character strengths

[49] Yet in their drive towards a development of practical applications the positive psychology movement may yet rely on the categorisation as a theory, get lost in semantics, reductionism or simplifying assumptions as Trait permanence.

[50] Reference the Research of Mischel, Variations with Situation. There is essentially no dimension of behaviour which is not both environmentally and genetically influenced. Whilst there is a wealth of research supporting the heritability of key personality traits there is too much interrelation between genes and environment and the hundreds of genes within themselves to be meanigful. The argument that genes play a great role in forming character traits -- such as self-control, decision making, aggression or sociability is misleadingly simplistic.

> "The scientific mistake is the familiar assumption of strong genetic determinism, with the unsupportable conclusion that two individuals with identical genomes will exhibit identical phenotypic expression. Not so. On the basis of the significant physical and behavioural differences found between identical twins, as well as for the multitude of reasons, it seems a near certainty that even genetically identical clones would exhibit very

different traits!" Pence G: Who's Afraid of Human Cloning? 1998, Lanham: Rowman and Littlefield

The heritability of (or genetic influence on) a trait does not mean that the trait itself is genetically determined. There are very few circumstances where free will plays little or no role in what we do.

[51] W. Fleeson, J. Wilt (2010) The Relevance of Big Five Trait Content in Behaviour to Subjective Authenticity: Do High Levels of Within Person Behaviour Variability Undermine or Enable Authenticity Achievement? Journal of Personality 78:4, August 2010

[52] And the introvert may see themselves as being closer to their authentic happy self when, on occasion, they may be the life of the party. An Individual's self-concept is not always straight forward.

[53] Consider the Milgram and Zimbardo experiments which caused controversy in the 1960s, coming, as they did, at a time when it was widely held that moral behaviour was a matter of individual responsibility (and not partly circumstantial). They demonstrated the importance of a situation. The situation changed ordinary American Undergraduates' behaviours to show unpredictable brutality. Zimbardo's Stanford prison experiment (SPE) was an attempt to investigate the psychological effects of perceived power, focusing on the struggle between prisoners and prison officers. Milgrams study concerned obedience that involved administering possibly fatal electric shocks. The conclusion remained largely the same: in certain situations, most ordinary people could be induced, quite readily, to behave badly. Behaviour had little to do with perceived character traits.

[54] Haydon 2006

[55] Bavarian N. et al. (2013) A Hawiian School Health study evaluated the impact of Positive Action (a social-emotional and character development programme) on educational outcomes among low-income, urban youth. It was found to influence academic outcomes among students living in low-income, urban communities. The programme significantly improved growth in academic motivation; mitigated disaffection with learning; had a positive

impact on absenteeism and a marginally significant impact on maths
performance of all students.

56 *The programme was called "Positive Action" and is an example of*
adjusting self-perception through action. It is based on the intuitive
philosophy that we feel good about ourselves when we do positive actions.
The Thoughts-Actions-Feelings Circle (TAF) illustrates how this works in
life: our thoughts lead to actions and those actions lead to feelings about
ourselves which in turn lead to more thoughts. When this cycle is positive,
students want to learn. When this cycle is negative, students do not want to
learn. The essence of the program is to emphasize those actions that promote
a healthy and positive cycle.

57 *In the test the researcher would present a child with a marshmallow and*
tell her that she could either eat one immediately or wait alone in the room
for several minutes until the researcher returned, at which point she could
have two Marshmallows.

58 *Roy Baumeister, a professor of psychology at Florida State University who*
studies willpower, put it, self-control is like a muscle: the more you use it,
the stronger it gets. https://www.newyorker.com/science/maria-
konnikova/struggles-psychologist-studying-self-control

59 *The new studies have shown that three basic aspects of personality change*
little throughout life: a person's anxiety level, friendliness and eagerness for
novel experiences. But other traits, such as alienation, morale and feelings of
satisfaction, can vary greatly as a person goes through life. These more
changeable traits largely reflect such things as how a person sees himself and
his life at a given point, rather than a basic underlying temperament.
http://www.nytimes.com/1987/06/09/science/personality-major-traits-found-
stable-through-life.html?pagewanted=all&mcubz=1

60 *This was a significant challenge and as a result the field of moral*
psychology was abandoned by personality and social psychology in the 1970s
because of the illusory nature and lack of stability in expected personality

characteristics (see Mischel 2004 in the Personality section for a historical review).

[61] *A Cognitive-Affective System Theory of Personality Reconceptualizing Situations, Dispositions, Dynamics, and Invariance in Personality Structure* https://psychology.columbia.edu/sites/default/files/2016-11/246.pdf

[62] *Moral Psychology, Chuck Huff, Owen Gaasedelen* http://www.oxfordbibliographies.com/view/document/obo-9780199828340/obo-9780199828340-0038.xml

Alan Batt (2015) "Teaching and evaluating the affective domain in Paramedic education" in Canadian Paramedicine, Voluime 38, Issue 1.

Fiest, G. J. & Fiest, J. (2008) Theories of Personality 7th Ed. McGraw Hill.

Friedman, H.S. & Schustack, M.W. (1999) Personality: Classic Theories and Modern Research Allyn & Bacon.

[63] Peter Salovey and John D. Mayer, "Emotional Intelligence," Imagination, Cognition, and Personality, 9, no.3 (1990): 185-211.

[64] *An EI-Based Theory of Performance, From the book The Emotionally Intelligent Workplace, Edited by: Cary Cherniss and Daniel Goleman* http://www.eiconsortium.org/pdf/an_ei_based_theory_of_performance.pdf

[65] *In analysing research findings across ninety-six studies, Hattie et al (1997) concluded that the greatest effects from Outdoor Adventure programmes relate to a sense of control over or regulation of the self, responsibility, or an assurance of self. self-control. Specifically, these included behaviours of independence, confidence, self-efficacy, self-understanding, assertiveness, internal locus of control, and decision making.*

[66] *The term condition is used cautiously and is not to be associated with behaviourism's conditioning- Learning here is not autonomous like Pavlov's dogs! But behaviour changes on the basis of learned expectations. People learn to predict events and to summon up anticipatory reactions - as we learn from the consequences. Albert Bandura (1974) "Behavior Theory and models of man" American Psychologist 859.*

[67] https://www.uky.edu/~eushe2/Bandura/Bandura1974AP.pdf

[68] *In conditioning us for elevation and Moral Action we should perhaps consider the Theory of Choice when weighing up the Tipping points*

[69] *In reflecting on our personal qualities, we address how we may engage with the world. It is not a matter of simply building character but rather in coaching and practising the skills of reasoning and reaction that condition our action in for the variability in situations. This is not new, Aristotle said character arises from the continual practice of virtues.*

[70] *Robert M. Pirsig, 1974: Zen and the Art of Motorcycle Maintenance: An Inquiry into Values*

[71] *Psychology Today*
http://youarenotsosmart.com/2010/10/27/procrastination

[72] *Thich Nhat Hanh, (1996) Living Buddha, Living Christ, Rider.*

[73] *William James (1890) as cited in Seligman, M. (1996). The optimistic child. New York : HarperCollins p.30*

[74]*Hasazi and Haszai, (1972) and Zimmerman and Zimmerman (1962)*

[75] *(Branson: 2007) How Not to Talk to Your Kids: The Inverse Power of Praise, New York Magazine, 12 February 2007.*

[76] *Meyer, W.-U. (1992). Paradoxical effects of praise and criticism on perceived ability. European Review of Social Psychology, 3, 259–283*

[77] *Baumeister, Campbell, Krueger, and Vohs (2005)*

[78] *Parents, grandparents, educators—everyone sends messages to children, whether they're aware of it or not. Praise for Intelligence Can Undermine Children's Motivation and Performance, Claudia M. Mueller and Carol S. Dweck, (1998) Columbia University*
Journal of Personality and Social Psychology 1998
1998, Vol. 75, No. 1, 33-52

[79] *Dweck, C. S. (1986). Motivational processes affecting learning. American Psychologist, 41(10), 1040-1048. p.1041*
https://www.sd27j.org/site/handlers/filedownload.ashx?moduleinstanceid=173&dataid=255&FileName=humanresources_c.pdf

[80] Dweck, Walton & Cohen, 2014 "Academic Tenacity, Mindset and skills that promote long term learning. " Gates Foundation

[81] Kamins, M., & Dweck, C.S. (1999).

[82] Concept of entity (Fixed) and incremental (Growth) attitudes.

[83] Dweck – in Arney's 2016, The problem with character education https://www.tes.com/news/school-news/breaking-views/problem-character-education

[84] Burhans and Dweck suggested that helplessness can result from a sense of contingent self-worth, such that when children feel they have failed, they think they are bad or unworthy, and this affects their responses to setbacks. By administering person- or trait-oriented feed- back (praise or criticism), adults may be teaching children that their competence, goodness, or worth is determined by their performance. Burhans, K.K., & Dweck,C.S.(1995).

[85] Dweck, C. S. (2007) Mindset: The New Psychology of Success

[86] Quote taken from Veevers (2006)

[87] Refers to Frederic Bartlett's work 1930..

[88] Anderson and Pichert,(1978).

[89] (Brookes A. 2006, p.163)

[90] Kahneman, D., & Deaton, A. (2010). High income improves evaluation of life but not emotional wellbeing. Proceedings of the National Academy of Sciences, 107, 16489-16493.

Kurtz, J. L. (2008). Looking to the future to appreciate the present: The benefits of perceived temporal scarcity. Psychological Science, 19, 1238-1241.

Quoidbach, J., & Dunn, E. W. (2013). Give it up: A strategy for combatting hedonic adaptation. Social Psychological and Personality Science, 4, 563-568

[91] Rorty, R. (1997) "Achieving our Country" Cambridge MA: Harvard Uni Press

[92] Dewey, J. (1920) "Reconstruction in Philosophy" Henry Holt & CO. : New York

[93] Emmons, R. A. (2007) "Thanks!" Boston: Ma; Houghton – Mifflin

199

[94] *The focus on reflection in experiential learning has been criticised for being too simplistic, reductionist and linear (Bell, 1993; Fenwick, 2003a; Fox, 2008; Holman et al., 1997; Roberts, 2008; Sawada, 1991). A major criticism of the experience - reflection binary is that it is another version of the Cartesian mind (cognitive reflection) - body (experience) split (Michelson, 1999).*

[95] *Bono, G., Emmons, R.A., Mc Cullough, M. (2004) "Gratitude in practice and the practice of gratitude" in p464 "Positive Psychology in Practice" Linley P.A. (2004) John Wiley & Sons: New York*

[96] *Emmons R.A. Mishra, A. (2010) "Why gratitude enhances wellbeing"*

[97] *http://www.etymonline.com/word/author*

[98] *Yet positivism has had relatively little influence on contemporary sociology or psychology; it encourages a misleading emphasis on superficial facts without any attention to underlying mechanisms that cannot easily be observed.*

[99] *(2014) Learning Space — Review of 'The Beautiful Risk of Education'*

[100] *Typically, solutions that prioritise the gaining of control effect a change that might either increase the distance in relationships or narrow them.*

PART THREE: HIGH IMPACT LEARNING

[101] *Pinar and Grumet's (1976)*

[102] *Yet in teaching we have the flipside of cultural learning. Teaching culture isn't as innate or natural. – (Joseph Henrich:2016, p52)*

[103] *Dewey, J. (1938/1997). Experience and education. Macmillan. Chapter 2, The Need of a Theory of Experience*

[104] *Tony Little, former headmaster at Eton in his book, An Intelligent Person's Guide to Education https://www.standard.co.uk/comment/comment/celebrate-alevels-then-remind-students-about-the-real-world-a3614011.html*

[105] *Durkheim, Moral Ethics Page 206,*

[106] *The Commission's board, consisting of high profile individuals, all resigned just prior to this reports publication, underlining the severity of their conclusions for the prospects of social mobility given the current state of the policy mix and national outlook.*

[107] *Sir Ken Robinson's very popular video from the RSA Academy supported by his book - (2016) Creative Schools: Revolutionizing Education from the Ground Up.*

[108] *- Ivan Illich (1971) Deschooling Society – Illich called for the use of advanced technology to support "learning webs" and self-directed education. He argued that institutionalised education was ineffective and leads to institutionalised society. "The current search for new educational funnels must be reversed into the search for their institutional inverse"*

[109] *It is now thought that only 100,000 years ago there were up to 6 other hominoids! Homo Neanderthals, Homo erectus, Homo Floresiensis, H. heidelbergensis, Homo antecessor & Homo sapiens. See Krause et al. in Nature, volume, 464, pages 894–897 (08 April 2010)*

[110] *Charles H. Hillman, Kirk I. Erickson & Arthur F. Kramer, (2008, in "Be smart, exercise your heart: exercise effects on brain and cognition"*

[111] *Shaun Gallagher's How the Body Shapes the Mind (2005), Andy Clark (1997) Alva Noë's Action in Perception (2004), Francesco Varela (1991) and Antonio Damasio (1994)*

[112] *The development of Hahn's vision had at its heart a foundation of philanthropy. Behind each school key benefactor, Prince Max von Baden, Sir Edward Dunbar, Lawrence Holt, Lord Kirkham, & more recently support from the Bill and Melinda Gates Foundation for expeditionary learning schools in the USA.*

[113] *Cheryl Dobbertin, <u>Urban Education with an Attitude</u> By Lauri Johnson, Mary E. Finn, Rebecca Lewis Cousins, Emily, Ed.; Mednick, Amy, 1999 Ed.Service at the Heart of Learning: Teachers' Writings.*

[114] *Flavin, 1996; Hahn, 1960*

[115] *Bell, B. (2012) Assessing the Effectiveness of an Adventure-Based First-Year Experience Class, Journal of College Student Development, Volume 53, Number 2, pp. 347-355 – also refers also to Chickering & Gamson, 1991; Kuh, Kinzie, Shuh & Whitt, 2005; Upcraft & Gardener, 1989.*

[116] *Pryor, Hurtado, Saenz, Santos, & Korn, (2007) The American Freshman: Forty Year Trends. Los. Angeles: Higher Education Research Institute, UCLA*

[117] *Flavin, M. (1996)*

[118] *Michael Gass & Simon Priest (1993) Using metaphors and isomorphs to transfer learning in adventure education Journal of Adventure Education and Outdoor Learning 10 4 18-23; also see Hovelynck (1998) Facilitating experiential learning as a process of metaphor development - Perspectives on metaphors in adventure education, http://www.outwardbound.fi*

[119] *Whether we like it or not, high-stakes examinations will remain a persistent feature of schooling- they provide the primary direction for schools. Without a deadline or standard to reach to, it could be (unfortunately) argued that a lot of the point of knowledge acquisition is lost. Yet, the tendency for high stakes assessments to distort the teaching process is everywhere. Most of the students are anxious and are afraid of failure. Teachers feeling under pressure to get progress in results, teach to the test.*

[120] *"Alleviating Learned Helplessness in a Wilderness Setting: An Application of Attribution Theory to Outward Bound", R. Newman (1980)*

[121] *'Adventure therapy' combined with cognitive-behavioral treatment for overweight adolescents, E Jelalian et. al. (2006) found that peer-based 'adventure therapy' was a promising adjunct to standard cognitive-behavioral weight control intervention for adolescents, and may be most effective for older adolescents.*

[122] *"Coping with Stress in Outdoor Recreational Settings: An Application of Transactional Stress Theory" Theron A. Miller Mc Cools (2010)*

[123] *Mike Brown (2009a) places learning, and observable change, within a socio-cultural frame rather than as primarily a function of cognitive*

processes within the individual. In "Reconceptualising outdoor adventure education: Activity in search of an appropriate theory." Australian Journal of Outdoor Education, 13(2), 3-13,

[124] *The situated and distributed nature of learning is largely ignored in Adventure Programming in favour of notions of individual growth and development. We should more carefully consider the context of students and relationships. "Who we are, or who we might become is inseparable from who we are with, where we are, and what we are doing" M. Brown, (2008). <u>Ongoing relationships</u> and a culture of practice are most important considerations. With the concept of Expeditionary Learning we pay respect to the situated nature of human activity and the importance of continuity of relationships in delivering impactful learning interventions.*

[125] *Although, the autonomous nervous system controls many of our body functions without any conscious input from us, (like breathing, digesting, and sleeping) we can do something that influences them, for example:*

- *Yawning is an automatic response to being tired , but we have a choice to sleep more.*
- *Headaches are an auto response to dehydration, but we have the choice to drink more.*

These auto responses are examples of our body's primitive intelligence, built into it from over the years of evolution. The examples show simply how we can still contribute to the creation of the conditions under which our biological systems function, leading to a significant impact on our experience.

[126] *Spinoza on Common Notions, From Interpreting Spinoza; Critical Essays (2008)*

[127] *Caspi, A. & Bem, D. (1990). Personality and change across the life course. In Lawrence Pervin (Ed.), Handbook of personality: Theory and research. New York: Guilford Press.*

[128] *Curriculum time pressures, performance league tables and insecure school leadership only exacerbates this.*

[129] "Extrinsic Rewards and Intrinsic Motivation in Education: Reconsidered Once Again" highlights that tangible rewards have a substantial undermining effect. Edward L. Deci, Richard Koestner Richard M.Ryan Review of Educational Research Spring 2001, VoL 71, No. 1, pp. 1-27

[130] Howard Adelman and Linda Taylor, UCLA, Student Engagement and Disengagement: An Intrinsic Motivation Perspective and a Mental Health Concern, Mental Health Promotion in Schools, 44-70
http://smhp.psych.ucla.edu/pdfdocs/intrinsic.pdf

[131] Ross & Nisbett (1991).

[132] Peter Benson's book "Sparks- How parents can help ignite the hidden strengths of teenagers" With The Search Institute, he did research with American teenagers. Here is a list of what were found to be the ten most common sparks. These were the activities and areas in which young people felt most alive, joyful and inspired:

> Creative Arts, Athletics, Learning (e.g. languages, science, history) Reading, Helping, serving, Spirituality, religion, Nature, ecology, environment, Living a quality life (e.g., joy, tolerance, caring), Animal welfare & Leading

[133] Professor Albert Bandura is Professor Emeritus of Social Science in Psychology at Stanford University. He has been a leading figure in psychology and education since the 1970's. His Social Learning Theory was one of his important contributions to education theory. In it, people learn from one another through social activities via observation, imitation, and modelling. Self-efficacy, self-regulation are key theoretical components of this theory which encompasses attention, memory, and motivation.

[134] Grusec, J.E. (1992). "Social learning theory and developmental psychology: The legacies of Robert Sears and Albert Bandura". Developmental Psychology, 28 (5), 776-786.Grabove 1997, pp. 90–91 See also Cranton (1994) and Taylor (1998) for a full discussion of these critiques.

[135] *This reciprocal relationship between Behaviour, personal factors and social environment is known as Bandura's Theory of Reciprocal Determinism.*

[136] *Storr, W. (2016)– A Better Kind of Happiness, New Yorker Article*

[137] *An important part of the Expeditionary Learning model is what is called "Crew". This is a group of 12 students who bond, support, discuss and meet daily as they journey through education. Crew provides a check-in on how the class is doing in terms of character and academic progress, and how well individuals are doing. It provides space to support relationship building among students and between adults and students (e.g., greetings, personal sharing, classroom discussions. Whenever possible, students in crew sit in a circle so they can see each other, participate actively in discussion, and hold each other accountable for high standards of character. Meetings follow clearly defined protocols that allow student voice and participation such as "Acknowledgements, Apologies and Making a Stand". School structures and traditions such as crew, community meetings, exhibitions of student work, and service learning ensure that every student is known and cared for, that student leadership is nurtured, and that contributions to the school and world are celebrated.*

[138] *Washington Heights Expeditionary Learning School or WHEELS as is commonly known. It is famous as it is one of the first EL (Expeditionary Learning) School and President Obama visited it praised its 100% success rate for getting students into college. WHEELS is at the top part of Manhattan in an area which is mostly Latino with some other cultures mixed in, there are no white Trump supporters around here. When you walk around the area you do get a sense of what the school has to contend with, drug use, low income families, parents who speak little English. So, for the area to have a high achieving school is a bonus and is having a ripple effect.*

[139] *McKinsey & Co McKinsey and Co. (2007) How the world's best performing school systems come out on top.*

[140] *Bonwell & Eison,(1991), Bonwell (2000)*

[141] Meyers, C., Jones, B.T. (1993) *Promoting active learning (first ed.)*. San Francisco: Jossey-Bass. p. xi.

[142] What is your priority as an educator? Is it primarily in progressing your career, in attaining credentials, or attending to your schools' performance in the beauty contest of league tables? Or is it in nurturing young minds and hearts? How your current actions align with true self concern is a matter of authenticity. Apart from being virtuous, personal authenticity is linked to wellbeing, self-esteem, positive affect, hope for the future, creativity, quality of relationships-.all which bring out the best in a leader!

[143] involvement in community-based projects would provide rich opportunities from which student can connect with personal values, grow in self efficacy and develop character through exercising virtues.

[144] Views championed by ideological authors

[145] Professor Leon Feinstein's article "On genetics and social mobility: why Toby Young's structural inequality argument is not science".
http://blogs.lse.ac.uk/politicsandpolicy/on-genetics-and-social-mobility/

[146] Larry Rosenstock is Founder of High Tech High, was director from 1996-1997 of the New Urban High School Project, an effort funded by the U.S. Department of Education to find and describe new models for urban high schools. Rosenstock and his team created three design principles that seemed to be common in the successful urban high schools. These design principles are:- personalization, real-world connection, and common intellectual mission.

Ron Berger is Chief Academic Officer of EL Education – Author of *An Ethic of Excellence*, He works with the national character education movement to embed character values into the core of academic work. works closely with the Harvard Graduate School of Education, where he teaches a course that uses exemplary student work to illuminate standards. He is an Annenberg Foundation Teacher Scholar and received the Autodesk Foundation National Teacher of the Year award.

REFERENCES

Adler, A. (1931/1992). What Life Could Mean to You. Oxford: Oneworld.

Adler, M. G. & Fagley, N. S. (2005). Appreciation: Individual differences in finding value and meaning as a unique predictor of subjective wellbeing. Journal of Personality, 73(1), 79-114.

Agate, Joel, (2010). "Inspiring Awe in the Outdoors: A Mechanistic and Functional Analysis" PhD Dissertations. Paper 607.

Agate J R., Ward W, (2012) Awe as a Catalyst for Enhanced Outdoor Learning Southern Illinois University Carbondale. Coalition for Education in the Outdoors Eleventh Biennial Research Symposium

Ainslie, G. (2005) "Emotion as a Motivated Behaviour", Veterans Affairs Medical Center, Coatesville and Temple.

Algoe, S. B., & Haidt, J. (2009). Witnessing excellence in action: The "other-praising" emotions of elevation, gratitude, and admiration. Journal of Positive Psychology, 4, 105–127

Allison, P., Carr, D and Meldrum, G. (2012) "Potential for excellence: interdisciplinary learning outdoors as a moral enterprise" The Curriculum Journal, 23:1, pp43 – 58Annas, J. (2011) Intelligent Virtue. Oxford: Oxford University Press

Anderson, R.C., and Pichert, J. 1978. Recall of previously unrecallable information following a shift in perspective. Journal of Verbal Learning and Verbal Behavior 17:1-12.

Aquino, K., & Reed, A., II. (2002). The self-importance of moral identity. Journal of Personality and Social Psychology, 83, 1423–1440

Aquino, K., Mc Ferran, B., Laven, M, (2011) Moral Identity and the Experience of Moral Elevation in Response to Acts of Uncommon Goodness, Journal of Personality and Social Psychology, Vol. 100, No. 4, 703–718

Arney, K. (2016), The problem with character education. Times Education Suppliment. 18 September 2016. https://www.tes.com/news/school-news/breaking-views/problem-character-education

Arthur, J., Kristjánsson, K., Harrison, T., Sanderse, W., Wright, D. (2017) Teaching Character and Virtue in Schools. London: Routledge.

Arendt, H. (1958) The Human Condition. Chicago: University of Chicago Press

Ashley, M. (2006). Finding the right kind of awe and wonder: The metaphysical potential of religion to ground an environmental ethic. Canadian Journal of Environmental Education, 11, 88-99.

Averill, J., Stanat, P., & More, T. (1998). Aesthetics and the environment. Review of General Psychology, 2, 153-174.

Baumeister, Bratslavsky, Finkenauer, & Vohs, 2001 "Bad Is Stronger Than Good" Review of General Psychology Vol. 5. No. 4. 323-370

Bavarian, N., Lewis, K. M., DuBois, D. Acock,A. Vuchinich, S.,Silverthorn,N., Snyder, F., Day, J. ,Ji, P.. Flay, B. (2013) Using Social-Emotional and Character Development to Improve Academic Outcomes: A Matched-Pair, Cluster-Randomized Controlled Trial in Low-Income, Urban Schools, Journal of School Health, Volume 83, Issue 11, November 2013, Pages 771–779]

Beames, S., Brown, M. (2016) Adventurous learning: A pedagogy for a changing world, Routledge.

Bem, D. J. (1965). An experimental analysis of self-persuasion. Journal of Experimental Social Psychology, 1(3),

Benson, P. (2008) Sparks: How Parents Can Ignite the Hidden Strengths of Teenagers, Jossey Bass.

Bettner, L. & Lew, A. (1990) Raising kids who can, Newton Centre, MA: Connexions Press

Berger, R. (2003) An Ethic of Excellence: Building a Culture of Craftsmanship with Students, Heinemann Educational Books.

Berger, R., Woodfin, L., Vilen, A., Mehta, J. (2016) Learning That Lasts: Challenging, Engaging, and Empowering Students with Deeper Instruction. Jossey-Bass.

Biesta, G., (2016) Reconciling ourselves to reality: Arendt, education and the challenge of being at home in the world Journal of Educational Administration and History Volume 48, 2016 - Issue 2: pp 183-192

Biesta, G., (2014) Beautiful Risk of Education: (Interventions Education, Philosophy, and Culture) Boulder and London, Paradigm

Bonington, C. (1966) " I Chose To Climb", Gollancz

Bono, G., Emmons, R.A., Mc Cullough, M. (2004) "Gratitude in practice and the practice of gratitude" in p464 "Positive Psychology in Practice" Linley P.A. (2004) John Wiley & Sons: New York

Bonwell, C, Eison, J.A. (1991), Active Learning: Creating Excitement in the Classroom. 1991 ASHE-ERIC Higher Education Reports. p. 2

Bonwell, C.(2000) Active Learning: Creating Excitement in the Classroom.https://www.ydae.purdue.edu/lct/hbcu/documents/Active_Lear ning_Creating_Excitement_in_the_Classroom.pdf

Brendtro, L., Brokenleg, M., Van Bockern, S. (1990). Reclaiming Youth at Risk: Our Hope for the Future. Bloomington, Solution Tree. http://larrybrendtro.com/

Brookes, A. (2003) A critique of neo-Hahnian outdoor education theory. Part one: Challenges to the concept of "character building" Pages 49-62 Journal of Adventure Education and Outdoor Learning Volume 3, 2003 - Issue 1

Brown, M. (2008). Outdoor education: Opportunities provided by a place-based approach. New Zealand Journal of Outdoor Education, 2(3), 7-25.

Brown, M. (2009a) "Reconceptualising outdoor adventure education: Activity in search of an appropriate theory." Australian Journal of Outdoor Education, 13(2), 3-13,

Brown, M. (2009b) "Out of the head and into the world: Situated perspectives on learning." Paper presented at 'Outdoor education research and theory: critical reflections, new directions', the Fourth International Outdoor Education Research Conference, La Trobe University, Beechworth, Victoria, Australia, 15-18 April 2009.

Burhans, K.K., & Dweck,C.S.(1995). Helplessness in early childhood: The role of contingent worth. Child Development, 66, 17191738

Burke, Edmund (1756) "A Philosophical Enquiry into the Origin of Our Ideas of the Sublime and Beautiful"

Carbonneau, N., Vallerand, R. J., Fernet, C., & Guay, F. (2008). The role of passion for teaching in intrapersonal and interpersonal consequences. Journal of Educational Psychology, 4, 977-987.

Carson, R. (1956). The sense of wonder. New York: Harper & Row.

Chang, S.-M. (2016,) The development and implementation of life education in Taiwan: A meaning-cantered positive education. Invited paper presented at the 9th Biennial International Meaning Conference in Toronto, ON.

Chawla, L. (1990). Ecstatic places. Children's Environments Quarterly, 7(4), 18-23.

Clarke, Jon (2016) "The Impact of Expeditionary Learning Schools in Inner City areas in the USA", Winston Churchill Memorial Trust Fellowship Report

Coleman, T.C. (2014). Positive emotion in nature as a precursor to learning. International Journal of Education in Mathematics, Science and Technology, 2(3), 175-190

Cobb, E. (1977). The ecology of imagination in childhood. New York: Columbia University Press.

Coker, G. (2012) "Building Cathedrals: The Power of Purpose" http://www.thecathedralinstitute.com/2012/05/13/the-recovering-bricklayer/

Cooper, G. (1994) The Role of Outdoor Education in Education for the 21st Century. The Journal of Adventure Education and Outdoor Leadership, 11(2), 9-12.

Csikszentmihalyi M (1998) The flow experience and its significance for human psychology. Cambridge University Press. pp. 15-35

Damon, W (2008) The Path to Purpose: Helping our children find their calling in life. New York: Free Press

de Saint-Exupéry, A. (1943). The Little Prince. Orlando: Harcourt Books.

Dewey J. (1916). Democracy and Education: An Introduction to the Philosophy of Education. New York: Macmillan.

Dewey J. (1920) "Reconstruction in Philosophy" Henry Holt & Co.: New York

DIdau, D. (2013) Improving peer feedback with Public Critique.
http://www.learningspy.co.uk/assessment/improving-peer-feedback-with-public-critique/

Durkheim, E (1961) Moral Education: A Study in the Theory and Application of the Sociology of Education. Translated by E. K. Wilson and H. Schnurer. New York: The Free Press

Dweck, C. S. (1986). Motivational processes affecting learning. American Psychologist, 41(10), 1040-1048. p.1041

Dweck, C.S. (1999). Self-theories: Their role in motivation, personality and development, Philadelphia, PA: Psychology Press.

Dweck, C. S. (2007) Mindset: The New Psychology of Success, Robinson

Dweck, Walton & Cohen, (2014) "Academic Tenacity, Mindset and skills that promote long term learning". Gates Foundation

Eisenberg, N. (2000). Emotion, regulation, and moral development. Annual Review of Psychology, 51, 665–697.

Ekman, P. (1992). An argument for basic emotions. Cognition & Emotion, Volume 6, 169–200. Issue 3-4

Emmons, R. A. (2007) "Thanks!" Boston: Ma; Houghton – Mifflin

Emmons R.A. Mishra, A. (2011) "Why gratitude enhances wellbeing" In Designing Positive Psychology, pp.248-262

Evans, G. W. and Fuller-Rowell, T. E. (2013), Childhood poverty, chronic stress, and young adult working memory: the protective role of self-regulatory capacity.

Evans, G. W. and Kim, P. (2013), Childhood Poverty, Chronic Stress, Self-Regulation, and Coping. Child Dev Perspect, 7: 43–48.

Flavin,M. (1996) Kurt Hahn's schools and legacy (Wilmington, Middle Atlantic Press

Fleeson and Wilt (2010) The Relevance of Big Five Trait Content in Behaviour to Subjective Authenticity: Do High Levels of Within Person Behaviour Variability Undermine or Enable Authenticity Achievement? Journal of 4, August 2010

Foley, M 92011) *The Age of Absurdity: Why Modern Life Makes It Hard to Be Happy*, Simon & Schuster

Friedman, H.S. & Schustack, M.W. (1999) Personality: Classic Theories and Modern Research Allyn & Bacon.

Fredrickson, B. L. (2000). Cultivating positive emotions to optimize health and wellbeing. Prevention and Treatment, 3, Article1.

Gallagher, S. (2006) How the Body Shapes the Mind, Oxford University Press Canada, ISBN-13: 9780199204168

Gilligan, C. (1982) In a different voice: Psychological theory and women's development. Cambridge, MA: Harvard University Press.

Goleman, D. (1996) Emotional Intelligence: Why it Can Matter More Than IQ. Bloomsbury Publishing PLC; New edition

Goodman, A., Joshi, H., Nasim, B., Tyler, C. (2015). Social and emotional skills in childhood and their long-term effects on adult life. Institute of Education, University College London.

Gordon, A. M., Stellar, J. E., Anderson, C. L., McNeil, G. D., Loew, D., & Keltner, D. (2017). The dark side of the sublime: Distinguishing a threat-based variant of awe. Journal of Personality and Social Psychology, 113(2), 310-328.

Greenaway, R. (2008) A View into the Future: The Value of Other Ways of Learning and Development: pp347-357 in Becker, P.& Schirp, J. (Eds), 2008 Other Ways of Learning, The European Institute for Outdoor Adventure Education and Experiential Learning 1996-2006, Marburg ISBN 978-3-940549-07-7

Haggis, T. 2008. "'Knowledge must be contextual': Some possible implications of complexity and dynamic systems research for educational research". In Complexity theory and the philosophy of education (pp. 150--168), Edited by: Mason, M. Chichester: Wiley-Blackwell.

Hahn, K. (1934). The practical child and the bookworm. The Listener November 28.

Hahn, K. (1958) Address at the Forty-Eighth Annual Dinner of Old Centralians, London. Journal of old Centralians 119, 3-8,

Hahn, K. (1960) The moral equivalent of war, Address at the Annual Meeting of the Outward Bound Trust (20 July) London: Outward Bound Trust.

Hahn, K. (1965) Harrogate address on Outward Bound. London: Outward Bound Trust. http://www.kurthahn.org/writings/

Haidt, J. (2000) "The Positive Emotion of Elevation "Prevention & Treatment, Volume 3, Article 3, posted March 7, 2000

Haidt, J. (2003). Elevation and the positive psychology of morality. In C. L. M. Keyes & J. Haidt (Eds.) Flourishing: Positive psychology and the life well-lived. Washington DC: American Psychological Association. (pp. 275-289).

213

Haidt, J. (2003). The moral emotions. In R.J. Davidson, K.R. Scherer, & H.H. Goldsmith (Eds.), Handbook of
affective science (pp. 852–870). Oxford, UK: Oxford University Press.

Haidt, J. (2006). The happiness hypothesis: Finding modern truth in ancient wisdom. New York: Basic Books

Halstead, J. & Halstead, A. (2004). Awe, tragedy and the human condition. International Journal of Children's Spirituality, 9(2), 163-175

Haralambos, M. and Holborn M. (2008)– Sociology Themes and Perspectives - ISBN 10: 0007245955 - Collins Educational

Harrison, T., Morris, I., Ryan, J. (2016) Teaching Character in the Primary Classroom, Sage Publications Ltd

Hart, T. (2005). Spiritual experiences and capacities of children and youth. In E. C. Rhehlkepartain, P. E. King, l. Wagener,and P. L. Benson (Eds.). The Handbook of Spiritual Development in Childhood and Adolescence, pp. 163-178. Thousand Oaks: Sage Publications

Hasazi, Joseph E., and Susan E. Hasazi. "Effects of Teacher attention on digit-reversal behavior in an elementary school child." Journal of Applied Behavior Analysis 5.2 (1972): 157-62.

Hattie, J., (1999, June.) Influences on student learning (Inaugural professorial address, University of Auckland, New Zealand). Retrieved from https://cdn.auckland.ac.nz/assets/education/hattie/docs/influences-on-student-learning.pdf

Hattie, J., Marsh H. W., Neill J.T., Richards G.E. (1997) Adventure Education and Outward Bound: Out-of-Class Experiences That Make a Lasting Difference. Review of Educational Research 67: 43

Heintzman, P. (2006). Men's wilderness experience and spirituality: A qualitative study. Northeastern recreation research symposium.
Heschel, A. (1983). I asked for wonder. Chestnut Ridge, NY: Crossroad Publishing.

214

Hircsh E.D. (1988) Cultural Literacy: What Every American Needs to Know, Random House USA Inc;

Hopkins, D. and Putnam, R. (1993) Personal Growth through Adventure. London: David Fulton.
International Baccalaureate. 2008. Creativity, action, service guide, Cardiff: International Baccalaureate Organization.

Johnson, B. (2002). On the spiritual benefits of wilderness. International Journal of Wilderness, 8(3), 28-32.

James, W. (1983). The principles of psychology. Cambridge, MA: Harvard University Press. (Original work published 1890)

Jarvis, P. (2012) "Learning to be a person in society" Ch2 in Contemporary Theories of Learning, Knud Illeris (2009), Routledge. P26.

Jelalian, E., Lloyd-Richardson, E.E., Birmaher V.,Wing R. R. (2006) 'Adventure therapy' combined with cognitive-behavioural treatment for overweight adolescents. International Journal of Obesity volume 30, pages 31–39

John, K. (2011) Belonging & Significance, ASIIP Conference, Bath 29-30 April 2011, page 5. from http://www.adleriansociety.co.uk/

John, O.P. & Srivastava, S (1999) The Big Five trait taxonomy: History, measurement, and theoretical perspectives. In LA Pervin & OP John (Eds.) Handbook of personality: Theory and research (pp 102-138) New York: Guilford Press.

Jubilee Centre for Character and Virtues, (2017) A Framework for Character Education in Schools http://www.jubileecentre.ac.uk

Jubilee Centre for Character and Virtues and #1will Campaign: "Youth Social Action and Character Development". Birmingham Available: http://www.jubileecentre.ac.uk/userfiles/jubileecentre/pdf/Statem entSocialAction.pdf (accessed August 2017].

Jubilee Centre for Character and Virtues, (2017) A Habit of Service http://www.jubileecentre.ac.uk/

Kahneman, D., & Deaton, A. (2010). High income improves evaluation of life but not emotional wellbeing. Proceedings of the National Academy of Sciences, 107, 16489-16493

Kahneman, D. (2011) Thinking, Fast and Slow, New York: Farrar, Straus and Giroux.

Kagan, J. 1998. Three seductive ideas, Cambridge, Massachusetts: Harvard University Press

Kamins, M., & Dweck, C.S. (1999). Person vs. process praise and criticism: Implications for contingent self-worth and coping. Developmental Psychology, 35, 835–847.

Kant, I (1764) Beobachtungen über das Gefühl des Schönen und Erhabenen – Observations on the Feeling of the Beautiful and Sublime. University of California Press; 2nd Revised edition edition (27 Jan. 2004)

Kant, I. (1959). Foundations of the metaphysics of morals (L. W. Beck, Trans.). New York, NY: Bobbs-Merrill.

Keltner, D, Haidt, J. (2003) Approaching awe, a moral, spiritual and aesthetic emotion, Cognition and Emotion 17(2) 297-314

Keltner, D. (2009). Born to be good: The science of a meaningful life. New York: W. W. Norton & Company.

Keltner, D., Lerner, J. S. (2010). Emotion. In Fiske, S. T., Gilbert, D. T., Lindzey, G. (Eds.), Handbook of social psychology (pp. 317–352). Hoboken, NJ: John Wiley & Sons.

Keltner, D. (2012) "Generation Wii… or Generation We?" Graduation Address, University of California, Berkeley. http://greatergood.berkeley.edu/

Kamins, M., & Dweck, C.S. (1999) Person Versus Process Praise and Criticism: Implications for Contingent Self-Worth and Coping Developmental Psychology, Vol. 35, No. 3, 835-847

Kirk J. Schneider (2008) Rediscovering Awe: A New Front in Humanistic Psychology, Psychotherapy, and Societ, Canadian Journal of Counselling /

Kirkman, E., Sanders, M., Emanuel, L. and Larkin, C. (2015). Evaluating Youth Social Action: Does Participating in Social Action Boost the Skills Young People Need to Succeed in Adult Life. London: Behavioural Insights-Team

Kirschner, P.A., Sweller, J. (2006) Why Minimal Guidance During Instruction Does Not Work: An Analysis of the Failure of Constructivist, Discovery, Problem-Based, Experiential, and Inquiry-Based Teaching, Educational Psychologist , 41(2), 75–86

Kohlberg, L. (1969). Stage and sequence: The cognitive developmental approach to socialization. In D. A. Goslin (Ed.), Handbook of socialization theory (pp. 347–480). Chicago, IL: Rand McNally.

Kristjánsson, K. (2017) Aristotelian Character Education. London: Routledge.

Kristjánsson, K. (2013) 'Ten Myths about Character, Virtue and Virtue Education - and Three Well-Founded Misgivings', British Journal of Educational Studies , vol. 61, no. 3, pp. 1-19.

Kurtz, J. L. (2008). Looking to the future to appreciate the present: The benefits of perceived temporal scarcity. Psychological Science, 19, 1238-1241.

Lazarus, R. (1991). "Cognition and Motivation in Emotion," American Psychologist, 46: 362–67.
LeDoux, J., (1998). The Emotional Brain: The Mysterious Underpinnings of Emotional Life, New York: Simon and Schuster.

Lilley, T. (1998) Outdoor Adventure Education with Young People at Risk in Higgins and Humberstone (1999) Outdoor Education and Experiential Learning in the U.K. p. 50

Loynes, C. (1998) Adventure in a bun Journal of Experiential Education 21 (1), 35-39, 1998

Long, K. (2015) An Outdoor Educators Guide to Awe, The Outward Bound Trust, Penrith

McKenzie, M. 2003. Beyond 'the Outward Bound process': Rethinking student learning. Journal of Experiential Education, 26(1): 8–23.

Mani, A. Mullainathan, S., Shafir E., Zhao, J. (2013) Poverty Impedes Cognitive Function, Science 30 Aug 2013: Vol. 341, Issue 6149, pp. 976-980 DOI: 10.1126/science.1238041

Merleau-Ponty, M. (1962) Phenomenology of Perception, Routledge

Mezirow, J. (2000) "Learning as Transformation: Critical Perspectives on a Theory in Progress" San Francisco: Jossey Bass

Mortlock, C.(1984) The Adventure Alternative. Milnthorpe, Cumbria: Cicerone Press.

Narval, P, (2011) The Aristocracy of Service- The legacy of Kurt Hahn in the 21st Century" Uni Oxford, MSc Dissertation.

O'Brien, K. & Lomas T. (2017) Developing a Growth Mindset through outdoor personal development. Journal of Adventure Education and Outdoor Learning Vol. 17, 2

Olson, J. M., & Stone, J. (2005). The influence of behavior on attitudes. In D. Albarracín, B. T. Johnson, & M. P. Zanna (Eds.), The handbook of attitudes (pp. 223–271). Mahwah, NJ: Lawrence Erlbaum.

Ortony, A. (1988) "Subjective Importance and Computational Models of Emotions "Cognitive Perspectives on Emotion and Motivation pp 321-343

Peterson, C., & Seligman, M. E. P. (2004). Character strengths and virtues: A handbook and classification. New York: Oxford University Press and Washington, DC: American Psychological Association.

Piff, P. K., Dietze, P., Feinberg, M., Stancato, D. M., & Keltner, D. (2015). How awe promotes prosocial behavior through the small self. Journal of Personality and Social Psychology, 108, 883-899.

Piff, P. K., & Keltner, D. (2015). Why do we experience awe? The New York Times, p. SR10.

Pinar, W., Madeleine M. R. (1976) Toward a poor curriculum. Authors, Kendall/Hunt Pub. Co

Pirsig, R. M. (1974): Zen and the Art of Motorcycle Maintenance: An Inquiry into Values

Priest, S. (1990). The adventure experience paradigm. In J.C. Miles, & S. Priest (Eds.), Adventure Recreation. (pp.157-162). State College PA: Venture Publishing.

Proust M, *(1923) "Remembrance of Things Past; Vol. V, _The Captive" Ch. II (1929 C. K. Scott Moncrieff translation)

Quoidbach, J., & Dunn, E. W. (2013). Give it up: A strategy for combatting hedonic adaptation. Social Psychological and Personality Science, 4, 563-568

Reid, M.A., Barrington, H., (2004) Human Resource Development: Beyond Training Interventions P17.

Ross, L., & Nisbett, R. E. (1991). McGraw-Hill series in social psychology. The person and the situation: Perspectives of social psychology. New York, NY, England: Mcgraw-Hill Book Company.

Rousseau, Jean-Jacques, (1762.) Émile, or Treatise on Education, Prometheus Books; New edition (20 Aug. 2003)

Rorty, R. (1997) "Achieving our Country" Cambridge MA: Harvard Uni Press

Rudd, M., Vohs, K., & Aaker, S. (2012). Awe Expands People's Perception of Time, Alters Decision Making, and Enhances Wellbeing. Psychological Science.

Scherer, K. R. (1984). On the nature and function of emotion: A component process approach. In K. R Scherer & P. Ekman (Eds.). Approaches to emotion (pp. 293- 317). Hillsdale, NJ: Erlbaum

Schnall, S., Roper, J., & Fessler, D. M. T. (2010). Elevation leads to altruism, above and beyond general positive affect. Psychological Science, 21, 315–320

Schneider, (2008) Rediscovering Awe: A New Front in Humanistic Psychology, Psychotherapy, and Society
Canadian Journal of Counselling / Revue canadienne de counseling / 2008, Vol. 42:1 67

Schusterman, R. (2006) Thinking Through the Body, Educating for the Humanities: A Plea for Somaesthetics , The Journal of Aesthetic Education Volume 40, Number 1, Spring 2006 pp. 1-21

Sebba, R. (1991). The landscapes of childhood — The reflection of childhood's environment in adult memories and in children's attitudes. Environment and Behavior, 23(4), 395-422.

Seligman, M. & Csikszentmihalyi, M. (2000). Positive Psychology: An Introduction. *American Psychologist, January, 2000.* 55(1): 5-14

Shweder, R. A., Mahapatra, M., & Miller, J. (1987). Culture and moral development. In J. Kagan &: S. Lamb (Eds.), The emergence of momlity in young children (pp. 1- 83). Chicago: University of Chicago Press

Silvers and Haidt (2008) "Moral Elevation Can Induce Nursing", Emotion, Vol. 8, No. 2, 291–295

Smith, K, Cacioppo, J, Larsen, J & Chartrand, T. (2003). May I have your attention, please: Electrocortical responses to positive and negative stimuli. Neuropsychologia. 41. 171-83.

Shenk, D. (2010) The Genius in all of us – Why everything you've been told about genetics, talent and intelligence is wrong. Icon Books/ Random House , London.

Shiota, M. N., Keltner, D., & Mossman, A. (2007). The nature of awe: Elicitors, appraisals, and effects on self-concept. Cognition and Emotion, 21, 944-963.

Snyder, F.J., Vuchinich, S., Acock, A., Washburn, I. J. and Flay, B. R. (2012). 'Improving Elementary School Quality through the Use of a Social Emotional and Character Development Program: A Matched-Pair, Cluster Randomized, Controlled Trial in Hawaii', Journal of School Health, 82, 1, 11–20

Snyder, M. (1987) "Public appearances, private realities: The psychology of self-monitoring." New York, NY, US: W H Freeman/Times

Storr, W. (2016) "A Better Kind of Happiness" – New Yorker, July 7,

Taylor, A. (2017). Character Education: Bibliography of Recent Research, Reports and Resources. Slough: NFER.

Tannenbaum, R. & Schmidt, W. (1958) "How to choose a leadership pattern" Harvard Business Review 36(2), pp.95-101

van Oord, Lodewijk. (2010). Kurt Hahn's moral equivalent of war. Oxford Review of Education. 36. 253-265.

Vianelloa, M. Galliania EM, Haidt, J. "Elevation at work: The effects of leaders' moral excellence" The Journal of Positive Psychology Vol. 5, No. 5, September 2010, 390–411

Waters, M, (2013) Thinking Allowed: on Schooling, Crown House Publishing.

Williams, R. (2011) "The Impact of Residential Adventure Education on Primary School Pupils" Thesis for the degree of Doctor of Education, University of Exeter

Williams, R (2012) Woven into the fabric of experience: residential adventure education and complexity, Journal of Adventure Education and Outdoor Learning Volume 13, 2013 - Issue 2

Wilson, M, (2002) Six views of embodied cognition, Psychonomic Bulletin & Review 2002, 9 (4), 625-636

Wilson, R. A. (2008). Nature and young children — encouraging creative play and learning in natural environments. London: Routledge

Veevers, N. J. (2006) Your Disability is Your Opportunity: A historical study of Kurt Hahn focusing on the early development of outdoor activities. Masters Dissertation, University of Edinburgh Moray House School of Education.

Zak, P. Kurzban, R. & Matzner, W.T., (2005) Oxytocin is associated with human trustworthiness, Hormones & Behaviour, Dec;48(5):522-7. Epub 2005 Aug 18.

Zakrzewski V. (2013) "How Awe Can Help Students Develop Purpose", http://greatergood.berkeley.edu/

Zimmerman, E. H., & Zimmerman, J. (1962). The alteration of behavior in an elementary classroom. Journal of the Experimental Analysis of Behavior, 5, 50–60.

INDEX

223

Lightning Source UK Ltd.
Milton Keynes UK
UKHW042247171218
334165UK00001B/303/P

9 780954 778224